Life is too short ...

Life is too short ...
to miss today

Margaret Foth

Zondervan Publishing House
Grand Rapids, Michigan

Daybreak Books are published by Zondervan Publishing House, 1415 Lake Drive, S.E., Grand Rapids, Michigan 49506.

Library of Congress Cataloging in Publication Data

Foth, Margaret.
  Life is too short–.

  "Daybreak books."
  Bibliography: p.
  1. Conduct of life. 2. Christian life–1960- 3. Foth, Margaret. I.
Title.
BJ1581.2.F67   1985   248.4   85-8350

ISBN 0-310-42681-2

Edited by Linda Vanderzalm and Julie Ackerman Link

Printed in the United States of America

85 86 87 88 89 90 / 10 9 8 7 6 5 4 3 2 1

Contents

Reflecting Our Values

Life is too short ...

Introduction

"Dost thou love life? Then do not squander time, for that is the stuff life is made of," Ben Franklin observed two hundred years ago. Life is too short to waste on trivia, so celebrate life by loving freely and giving of yourself. I learned about celebrating life and using time wisely from a friend.

HER NAME WAS BETTIE. I had known her when we were both students in a small Mennonite college in Indiana. I knew her only as a quiet, serious, student musician. She played the cello.

Fifteen years later, I was married to Don, had four children, and lived in a suburb of Buffalo, New York. One afternoon a friend called to tell me that Bettie — Bettie from college acquaintance — was in Buffalo at Roswell Park Memorial Hospital, a cancer research center. I called to invite her to have dinner with us.

Now Bettie was walking toward me with outstretched hands and a smile of greeting that said, "Fifteen years of distance can't separate us!" As we ate dinner together, we all warmed to this charming, witty, loving woman. She accepted our invitation to make our home her "resting place" whenever she came to the hospital. She already knew that would be four times a year.

The cancer growing in Bettie was a rare one. The drugs prescribed were experimental, and the doctors could only tell her: "We can't predict your future. Some who have had this cancer have lived only a few months; others have lived five years."

Whenever Bettie came to Buffalo, our family celebrated life with her. On the first evening of her visits she would bring a gift for each of us — sometimes a book, once a set of pencils personalized with each child's name, a new record, a jigsaw puzzle, a scarf, or funny note paper. The gifts were not expensive, but they were always evidence of her finely tuned sensitivity. In turn we served her favorite foods, gathered flowers for her, and recalled the funny or sad stories we wanted to share. No one made dates to go out while Bettie was with us; no one wanted to miss any of the fun of playing and talking and reading together.

Bettie entered our family life during the period I recall as, "What have we done wrong?" Our four children teased, fought, and argued — far too much, I thought. Life was hectic. Every morning someone forgot either lunch, books, or home-work! Paydays came at least one week after the previous paycheck had been consumed. If I cleaned the house one morning, you couldn't see the difference by 5 P.M. And I was discouraged.

Bettie opened my eyes with her insight. She saw creativity in Ellen's drawings and cut-paper posters; she discussed Bob's new book about rockets and exclaimed over the insights of his reports; she heard the musical qualities of Mary's piano practice; she marveled at Jan's acrobatics — or whatever one of them happened to be trying at the moment! She saw individuality and growth; she saw humor and kind and thoughtful acts; she saw normal children — and complimented their parents, often and generously. And we all felt as if the sun had broken through after a rainstorm!

Bettie lived eleven years with cancer. She was taking chemotherapy treatments all that time, so she lived with about half her normal energy. But she taught her college music classes, counseled with students, and directed the Sunday school choir. And every afternoon she took time to rest, meeting her body's demands.

How does one plan for tomorrow when time is certainly limited? How does one choose what is more important when energy is limited? How does one *live* when there is only today?

Through ten years of visits we watched Bettie grow more and more confident and accomplished in loving. We watched her live joyfully, saw her smile through tears, heard words of hope emerge from depression.

And we weren't the only ones touched by Bettie. Her energy to love seemed unlimited. After Bettie died, a faculty colleague wrote: "Her cheerfulness and irrepressible good humor permeated our department and altered the texture of relationships. To function in such a way through eleven long years of chemotherapy seemed remarkable at the time. Somehow, in retrospect, it seems much more so. . . .

"When Bettie died, many noticed the evidence of faith that allowed her to die with such peace. I want to remember even more the evidence of faith that allowed her to live life with such uncommon grace."[1]

As a result of Bettie's time with us, I realized that our family self-image had changed. As I had received the gifts of love and appreciation from Bettie, I saw new choices and new priorities for myself. I didn't have the certain life deadlines that Bettie faced, but I also knew that I was given only one day at a time.

Each of us lives with the limitation of time. We cannot spend tomorrow just as we cannot buy back yesterday. Time forces us to choose: We have time enough to do only what is most important today.

Actually I think I've always had some sense that time is limited. One of my early recollections is of wanting to go to school, but my parents decided that I should not start first grade until I was almost seven. I was so unhappy — I was losing time. I would be a year late in learning to read! Finally I attended school, and I learned to read — but I still wanted more *time*. I wanted to read, and my mother wanted me to help with the housework. By the time I was twelve we came to an unvoiced compromise. Every Saturday morning I chose to "clean the upstairs." What that really meant was that I tucked my current book into the cleaning supplies as I climbed the stairs. After I noisily established the fact that I was cleaning, I stopped to read — "for a few minutes." Finally my mother would call exasperatedly, "Are you about finished with cleaning?"

"Not quite," I'd answer, shoving the book under the nearest mattress. Once in a while she even came up the stairs to see how I was doing. As I said, it was an unvoiced compromise. Now that I am a mother myself , I am sure that she knew it was much too quiet for any sweeping or dusting to be happening during that first hour.

I never seemed to have enough time. In college I didn't have time to take all the courses I wanted or to prepare for the debate tournament. While working as a newswriter, I always wanted to contact one more source or find another story, but the printing deadline cut me short. After I was married, I learned that my husband and I didn't even look at a clock with the same perception. When he looked at the time piece he said, "Time to be in the car and leaving!" But I was thinking, "Time to put the meat loaf in the oven before we go." Believe me, my husband and I have often discussed "time"!

After almost twenty years of mothering, part-time jobs in teaching, looking for work that fitted *me,* I was invited to begin a radio program for women. Was it "poetic justice" the program was named "Your Time"?

What had I learned about time? Particularly, what had I learned from knowing and watching Bettie? From my children growing up? From my parents growing old?

Time is the raw material of life. Time is very elusive, yet

exactly measured. Everyone has time. A minute or an hour is measured the same at any point in our earth. Time is given without discrimination to child or parent or grandparent, to governor or farmer, to secretary or salesperson. Yet all of us have known hours to fly and minutes to drag interminably. I remember my shock when I looked at the calendar exactly a month after the birth of our son. He had been born two weeks "late." I found it impossible to believe that it had been twice as long *since* his birth as those two endless weeks of waiting had been.

Time can be wasted or time can be filled. Time is an investment that pays dividends or slips into losses. From Bettie I learned to ask, "What is more important *now?*" I have many options for using my time; I need to say "no" to those activities that will have no lasting value, and I need to say "yes" to what is important.

I think that in North America we've been conned — or we've conned each other — into using time carelessly. We waste it in looking for happiness, forgetting that happiness comes as a by-product of loving and giving and working. We squander time in trying to keep our house as clean as our neighbor's or shopping when our closets are already full. We waste time in trying to keep a mask of respectability. We lose *today* while we look toward tomorrow or regret yesterday.

It is true that the way I use my time today will affect my future. What I'm doing now is building relationships, enlarging mental capacity, nurturing emotional depth — or dissipating my life energy.

Time is a gift of God from which we fashion a style of life, invest in loving relationships and work — work to provide for our own needs and to have full hands to offer to others. Time is the gift of God to "work out your own salvation," as the Apostle Paul reminds us, "for it is God who works in you to will and to act according to his good purpose" (Phil. 2:12, 13).

While I watched Bettie live out her time — she died at age

forty-five — I noted what she chose: time to listen to people and time to listen to God, time to give gifts, time to make music, time to enjoy meals with friends, time to write notes of affirmation and thanks, time to laugh and pray, time to cry, time to cheer the learning and developing beauty of her young friends. Those choices were affirmed by her growing faith and peace — God at work in her!

Recently I found a poignant poem called, "Life is too short . . ." by Doris Janzen Longacre. Doris wrote this shortly before she herself died from cancer. Her list of what life is too short for clarifies my own values and reminds me of those I saw Bettie choosing. And so this book brings together ideas for valuing time, for using time. You will, of course, need to make your own list. Bettie's, Doris's, my list — none will quite fit you.

Things That Life Is Too Short For

Life is too short to ice cakes.
Cakes are good without icing.
Life is too short to read all the church periodicals.
Life is too short not to write regularly to your parents.
Life is too short to eat factory-baked bread.
Life is too short to keep all your floors shiny.
It's too short to let a day pass without hugging your spouse and each of your children.
Life is too short to nurse grudges and hurt feelings.
It's too short to worry about getting ready for Christmas. Just let Christmas come.
Life is too short to spend much money on neckties and earrings.
It's too short for nosey questions like, "How do you like your new pastor?" or if there's been a death, "How is he taking it?"
It's too short to be gone from home more than a few nights a week.
It's too short not to take a nap when you need one.
It's too short to give importance to whether purses match shoes or towels match bathrooms.
It's too short to stay indoors when the trees turn color in fall, when it snows, or when the spring blossoms come out.
Life is too short to miss the call to worship on a Sunday morning.
It's too short for bedspreads that are too fancy to sleep under.
Life is too short to work in a room without windows.
Life is too short to put off Bible study.
It's too short to put off improving our relationships with the people that we live with.

Doris Janzen Longacre

Chapter 1

Life is too short ... to ice cakes

Or perhaps you prefer two-year-old John's version: "Icing is good without cake!" Either way, I want to choose what has weight and substance and integrity. I may not have time for the glamour of "icings."

RETURNING TO COLLEGE at age forty-one required courage. In the late sixties, I knew about the turmoil on college campuses because I watched news reports; I could guess how a middle-class woman with a middle-aged bulge would fit among the slim, long-haired, blue-jeaned youth. Having been a mother and homemaker for fifteen years, there was more "distance" than the miles between my house and the closest university! My "lessons" had included how to prepare dinner with tired and hungry children bugging me, how to glue a broken lampshade ten minutes before guests arrived, where to shop for shoes for children with narrow feet. . . . You get the picture?

However I wanted a graduate degree to teach English in high school, and that required returning to college. My husband and family encouraged me; they even made room in our budget for my tuition. Two of my friends had recently earned graduate degrees; I would not be the first to try. (They had graduated *cum laude* with perfect 4.0 averages!)

The morning I returned to campus, my knees felt like spaghetti. But I chose my courses and registered with a minimum of confusion. I even found a place to park regularly — an accomplishment on that city campus.

My first class was taught by a professor from India. He was a scholar with a delightful sense of humor (at least he laughed a lot) and an accent that made it difficult to understand him. I couldn't understand half! After the third class he announced a test, and *that* I understood. I hurried home to study — after all, I had to make an *A* to keep up with my friends and to prove to myself that I wasn't "too old"!

The test was a crisis for me. Studying had been complicated; one child had the flu and earache (with four children that wasn't too abnormal), and I knew I couldn't earn an *A* in this course. My head ached and my stomach hurt.

What was I doing in graduate school? Why did I begin? Should I drop out now rather than face further humiliation? All the while I was driving to class, my thoughts spun like a tire on ice. I parked and began the long walk, and my feet seemed to be cement blocks. Suddenly those questions stopped whirling as I had a flash of insight: "I don't *need* to have a perfect record! I don't have to earn an *A* today!" The cement blocks dropped off.

I finished that course (and didn't get an *A)*, but I realized in a new way that I could make choices that were good for *me.*

I couldn't change my instructor or the necessity of getting a degree if I wanted to teach, but I could choose a new image of myself. I did have the freedom to choose to balance personal needs with the needs of others. These classes were a necessary

Life is too short...

step toward teaching, and teaching would be one part of my life's work. My family was another part of my life, and I would go on caring for them when they had the flu — or when they were healthy! They came first; there was still room in my life for school and for a career with which I could make a contribution to society.

We Can Make Choices

When the way is frightening, when the tests are difficult, we feel breathless and trapped — without choices.

One day a friend called me to say she *had* to talk. When we met, the words spurted out: "My marriage is over — Marv moved out this morning — what will I do? I can't make it alone — how could he do this to me — *he's* made me into this woman he now finds 'uninteresting' and 'nagging.' My life is over! I don't have any choices — Marv made them — he's always made them."

Although she couldn't see her choices at that time, my friend really did have possibilities. She couldn't change her husband or the past (no matter how much she wished to). She couldn't change the necessity of moving out of the home she enjoyed. But whatever she did would be a choice. She would choose whether to brood in anger and bitterness or learn to forgive and nurture herself into health and strength. She would choose how to use her resources and her time.

I remember another point at which I made a conscious choice. Evening mealtime was becoming a contest of patience and wills between four children and two tired parents. And the tired parents were losing! Cooking was not my favorite job, and setting table was not anyone's welcomed interruption. By the time we dished up the hot food and scrambled to usual chairs, everyone was irritable — that was on our better nights! One afternoon I realized I was *dreading* dinner time. "Wait a minute," I thought. "There has to be some way to break the habits we're forming. Someone ends up crying every time!" I

to ice cakes

decided to try serving dinner in the dining room. We'd use our tablecloths and china and maybe candles once in a while. The girls would enjoy making the table look "pretty," and we could all bring our manners to match. One more advantage — the children's chairs could all be almost a foot apart!

And it helped. We started with different attitudes and we responded to the happier atmosphere. Of course, some of the newness wore off, but the old habits were changed.

Choices have a way of being made by default. We get up on the same schedule or watch TV on Saturday morning or buy groceries at the same store — without recognizing that we've made a choice. We use the same tone of voice when talking to Sara or Tom, call Merle on the phone every day, mentally turn off the kids' chatter — all without conscious choice. We cannot stop and agonize over each decision, but we can periodically look at directions and ask where our choices are taking us.

If we stop to think about them, today's choices may affect our children and grandchildren. For instance I once flipped light switches and turned up thermostats without hesitation. Now that I'm aware that electricity is produced by burning non-renewable resources — and our electric bills are climbing rapidly — I'm trying to make careful choices about using energy. I don't want to hand on a "burned-out" world to my great-grandchildren.

Most importantly, today's choices shape me, determining *how* I'll grow and change. The books and newspapers I read or don't read affect my thinking. The visits that I do or don't make to friends in the hospital shape me. The recreation I choose, the attitudes I take in work — however insignificant the momentary choice, each decision changes me. I become what I choose!

Guidelines for Choice

Through the years I've developed some guidelines to help me make choices. They are 1) what meets my needs, 2) what nurtures those for whom I have some responsibility, 3) what enhances values I believe are Christian.

Perhaps I need to explain why I put my own needs first. I do not choose to live *selfishly,* but I see the need to balance my well-being against the needs of others. I can't give responsibility for *me* to others. As one example of this tension: in places of severe food shortage, a mother must balance her need for food against the needs of her children. If she does not eat enough to keep herself active and alive, her children will certainly starve. I've seen mothers who are starving themselves *emotionally* or *mentally;* they have few resources to nourish those they claim to be "putting first."

In the past, women have been taught to let others make choices and take responsibility. Many young women moved from a home where "father knows best" — or at least made the decisions — to a marriage where husband expects — or is expected — to make the choices. In dating relationships women learned to wait — for the phone to ring, for a proposal, for someone else to make them happy. I believe we must take personal responsibility to mature into the persons we *can* be. To make choices based on my needs is to recognize that God has a purpose for me and wills that I grow into His image.

I also choose to nurture those persons for whom I have some responsibility, including my husband, children, and parents. Those are not necessarily simple choices. My parents are still able to live independently, but I know that within the next ten years, we will face difficult decisions. We will need to *care* for them. That may mean finding full-time nursing care or part-time housekeeping. We may need to make room in our home for them to live. When I was a child, grandpa lived with us for a few years. I remember him sitting in a rocking chair near a window where he could watch us as we played outside. My parents had to act as referees between their children's story and grandpa's version of what happened. The time came when grandpa needed to be moved to a home where he could have more nursing care. That was a painful parting, but it was a decision that balanced the needs within a family.

Each day we make choices that free or bind those we live with. Choosing to encourage, play with, listen to, hug, correct, work with, share with — each of these choices weaves into the life of each person strands that are incentives to grow or strands that bind.

The third guideline, choosing Christian values, is not really separate but the basis for all choices. I believe that Jesus taught us that "God is love." Therefore people are always valued over things. It is not occupation, appearance, wealth, or education that makes us lovable; rather our value comes from the potential image of God to be created uniquely in each of us.

Stereotypes and labels — racism, sexism, ageism — blind us to the infinite variety that could bless our lives. Choices come every time I meet another person: Shall I ignore the white-haired man who speaks out at the business meeting ("He doesn't know that the world is about anymore!")? Shall I allow my children to play with children of another race or faith? Shall I offer to hold a door open for the man in the wheelchair?

Once in a while we see a clear choice between right and wrong, but more often the moral values are fuzzy. Once in a while the decisions are weighty, requiring time and thought, but more often the consequences seem insignificant. We need to realize that all of our choices, whether weighty or insignificant, reflect our values. Does it make a difference if I buy a new coat this winter? Join the parent-teachers association? Walk, ride a bike, or drive a car? Join the book study or a card club? What are the implications of a decision to loan money to the man who needs it desperately but may not be able to repay? How will my choices affect me, my family, or the larger community of "children of God"? When we make these decisions, we need to learn to ask ourselves: How can my decision reflect what is really important to me?

Jesus talked about the rewards of those who choose to

feed the hungry, visit prisoners, care for the ill, or give a cup of water to the thirsty (Matt. 25:31–46). We serve God as we choose to share ourselves and what we have. Jesus was saying clearly that our choices have long-term consequences. But the choices are ours!

You can't control the length of your life —
    but you can control its width and depth.

You can't control the contour of your face —
    but you can control its expression.

You can't control the weather —
    but you can control the atmosphere of your mind.[1]

Caring for Ourselves

Chapter 2

Life is too short ...
to put off prayer and Bible study

"Your word is a lamp to my feet and a light upon my path."
Psalm 119:105

I'VE SEEN A POSTER that features a gigantic, single-edged razor blade. A man is stepping carefully on its edge, balancing in one hand a house and furnishings, in the other hand two cars and a boat and camper. The title of the picture is "Tension."

If you were to draw a picture of your tension, what things are you juggling? In one hand you have a house to care for, a family to feed and chauffeur; in the other hand you have a part-time job and a Sunday school class to teach. Or maybe your hands are filled with caring for aging parents as well as college-going children, all to balance against a salary that is shrinking with inflated costs of living.

We have conflicting interests and demands on our time and energy and finances. Juggling produces tension and stress.

We feel the effects of stress in headaches, arthritis, high blood pressure, and ulcers.

How can we handle these tensions? How can we love others when we are worrying about ourselves? How can we choose the "better" from among all the claims for attention and support? One woman said she feels like a jigsaw puzzle in five hundred pieces: she needs someone to put the pieces in order.

Dealing With Fears

Many people are finding that Christian meditation enables them to deal with fear and worry. In meditation, one can focus on the day. God promises what we need for today. What is most important? In the confusion of daily needs and problems it is helpful to ask, "What is the task for today?"

To practice Christian meditation we do not need to return to a past time or find another quieter place to live. The one quality necessary is commitment — a determination to make the effort — for we seek a discipline that will still the mind to truly meet God. Jesus used the words "a spring of water welling up to eternal life" to describe to one woman how God is within (John 4:14).

The "spring of water" is as effective a picture today as it was two thousand years ago. Picture a spring in the woods, bubbling up from among the fallen leaves; picture the spring coming from among the layers of rock on a mountainside; picture the spring in the desert, making a place for plants to grow in that hot and sandy place. Whatever your personal picture of a spring, it is sparkling, clear water coming to the surface from a hidden source, and it is unending.

Making Time for the Spring of Water

"Practicing the presence of God" were the words Brother Lawrence, a seventeenth-century monk, used to describe his meditation. He learned to tune his inner ear to be aware of God's presence all the while he worked among the clatter and

Life is too short...

bustle in the monastery kitchen. Most of us covet that sense of God's presence. Yet we can use a variety of means to personally move toward a continuous awareness of God's presence.

In his book, *The Art of Christian Meditation*, David Ray says: "A relaxed state of mind can keep you on top of stress and reduce harmful strain to a minimal level." He personally has found that he needs fifteen minutes for meditation early in each day, to achieve this "relaxed state of mind."[1]

The technique for meditation that Ray uses is based on words. Choose a word that reflects your needs. After choosing a word, write it on a three-by-five card and spend a few minutes finding a verse from the Bible that assures you of God's promise for you. Write that on the card also.

With this visual reminder, you can relax and focus on your word and the promise. Let God speak to you in that word.

Ray also gives specific helps for relaxing, patterns that start with head and neck and end with toes. Physical relaxation is necessary to control the effects of stress and to still the mind.[2]

Meditation is not going to take away all of life's stress; it is not a magic cure for life's problems. The problems remain to be dealt with. But meditation helps to bring order out of chaos; lights one step at a time; offers perspective on relative values and relationships.

Keeping A Journal

I have a friend, Mary Herr, who has learned to rise early in the morning for meditation. "Let me say that when a stay-a-bed like me can gladly rise up early," Mary says, "and when my waking thoughts really are of God, then I know that my experience is authentic."

Mary told how she learned to use writing — keeping a journal — as the discipline for her meditation:

I attended a retreat two summers ago where a large part of the time was spent in silence. Our task was "to encounter God," and I discovered that I lacked a framework for that assignment. The discipline of writing was one helpful tool I found. From that time on, I wrote. Each morning after I studied and listened, I responded in writing. I also learned to listen *as* I wrote. My written conversations with God moved from monologue to dialogue, and prayer came to life in me! Today my journal is where I most often find perspective and objectivity.[3]

Some form of writing, of keeping a journal, has been a longtime discipline for those looking for life's meaning. Our literature is enriched by the journals of Dag Hammarskjöld, George Fox, and Evelyn Underhill, to mention just a few.

But the real reason for keeping a journal is not to publish it — or even to share it with another person. It is the discipline to develop awareness of God's presence and perspective on your life. A journal is for yourself.

One English "keeper of a journal," Malcolm Smith, said that he kept a journal to ask his questions of God and then to write those answers as he learned them.

Again, Mary Herr says of her journals:

People often ask how I can believe that what I write in dialogue with God is really from Him. I respond that God comes to us naturally, and always has. Read the Psalms or Job or Abraham. Dialogue with God is nothing new.[4]

. A journal may be a mirror in which to see yourself, to reflect the shadows as well as the sunlight of your life, and to hold your friends with you in the loving presence of God.

Bible Study

I've read guides to daily meditation and envied those who write journals. I've tried to discipline myself to set aside a half-hour a day for meditation. To be honest, these have not worked for me. And I've felt guilty. What flaw in me, what lack of commitment!

However I really enjoy Bible study. While I was in college, I audited a study of the gospel of John. For the first time, I saw that John illuminated the identity of Jesus in a new way. I saw patterns — Jesus' teaching on the "bread of life" followed the evening when he fed five thousand with bread, for instance. And the seeds of hatred that led to Jesus' crucifixion grew out of the revolutionary understanding of God's love (revolutionary to the Pharisees, that is!). This study was exciting and lifechanging!

Even if I didn't set aside fifteen minutes each day for meditation, I could spend two hours with pen, paper, and the Gospel and be renewed in my spirit and understanding. This learning continues to make connections with daily insights.

Since then I've taken other courses of Bible study, and I've worked on comprehensive studies on my own. For me, a larger block of time to organize what I'm reading into outlines is exciting and helpful. I'm not at all sure this study replaces meditation, but I think that both are helpful.

A Rhythm of "Creative Pauses"

Anne Morrow Lindbergh, in her book *Gift From the Sea*, shares her insights found during a vacation of meditation:

> I began these pages for myself, in order to think out my own particular pattern of living, my own individual balance of life, work and human relationships. And since I think best with a pencil in my hand, I started naturally to write ... But as I went on writing and simultaneously talking with other women, young and old, with different lives and experiences, ... I found that ... in varying settings and under different forms, ... many women, and men, too, were grappling with essentially the same question as I, ... to evolve another rhythm with more

creative pauses in it, more adjustment to individual needs,
and new and more alive relationships to themselves as well
as others.[5]

Notice how Anne refers to meditation as "creative
pauses," pauses that give meaning to the activities that
surround them.

Another writer, Harold Rogers, describes meditation as "a
handful of quietness." "A handful of quietness is so little," he
says, "but the benefits derived from those moments will be so
wonderful that before long they will become a natural part of
life."[6]

Christian meditation and study have two results: first is a
growing peace within and finding the source of strength for
your own life (the "spring of water"); the second is increasing
sensitivity to the needs of other persons and a new world-view.
Jesus' coming was Good News for a world where oppression
and injustice and selfish greed made slaves of men and women.
The more I study the Bible, the more I see meaning in praying,
"Thy will be done on *earth* as it is in heaven."

Chapter 3

Life is too short ...
to miss a nap when we need one

A thing of beauty is a joy forever:
Its loveliness increases; it will never
Pass into nothingness; but still will
Keep
A bower quiet for us, and a sleep
Full of sweet dreams, and health, and quiet breathing.
                                                    — John Keats

THE NURSE WAS GIVING HELPFUL ADVICE to expectant mothers: "A new baby may disrupt your sleeping and eating patterns, but you'll soon adjust. . . ." My mind went into one of its own journeys as I remembered how difficult those two adjustments had been with baby number one.

Since mothering four babies filled ten years of my life, *that* was the experience that taught me that driving a car, loving my husband, taking an interruption in stride, thinking through finances, breaking into tears, being patient with a late repairman, holding a pen steady — whatever I was trying to do — was affected by whether I had eaten balanced meals and slept enough.

If I had known about some of the research on sleep and how loss of sleep affects us, I wouldn't have felt so guilty about trying to find time for a nap while our children were sleeping.

In New York City, back in 1959, Peter Tripp was a well-known disc jockey. To benefit the Polio Fund, he planned to stay awake for two hundred hours. Tripp set up a glass-walled booth on Times Square. Across the street in the Hotel Astor, a special testing center was set up with an impressive crew of psychologists, psychiatrists, and medical specialists.

Tripp was given a preliminary checkup, and his normal level of functioning was established. Then during each day of his marathon he submitted to a battery of medical and psychological examinations.

From the first night on he struggled with the overpowering desire for sleep. After two days his mind began to play tricks on him. He saw cobwebs in his shoes. Specks on the table looked like bugs. After four days — only halfway through his marathon — Peter couldn't handle more than two of the daily psychological tests. By six days the tests were torture. Even the alphabet baffled him. In the last two days he became disoriented, wondering who he was and where he was — yet somehow he pulled himself together every evening for his regular broadcast from 5 until 8 P.M. [1]

The Need for Sleep

The effects of sleeplessness on Peter Tripp's mental and physiological functions are dramatic evidence of how important sleep is to us. Not many of us will try to stay awake for eight days, but the consequences of prolonged periods of insufficient sleep do affect the lives of millions of people. Shift workers, new parents, college students, and soldiers in combat often show personality changes due to sleep loss. These

Life is too short...

changes can range from irritability and mental confusion to serious psychological problems and the onset of disease. Sleep problems can create havoc in family life. Parents know what a crying child can do to a night's sleep. When it goes on for weeks and months, the strain affects the whole family.

For a while it was believed that people really didn't need to spend so much time in sleep. Famous nonsleepers such as Thomas Edison and Benjamin Franklin were held up as models of what the rest of us *could* do if we could conquer our weakness for sleep. Some tried to adapt themselves to as little sleep as possible. Little "catnaps" scattered through a twenty-four-hour period was one suggestion.

Part of the problem is that we haven't understood the nature of sleep. Systematic sleep research is relatively new. As one writer puts it, "We have only begun to track some of the unseen forces that govern the rhythm of our lives . . . by which we wake or dream."[2]

Stages of Sleep

Research has identified different stages of sleep that we normally go through; each night we repeat the stages four or five times. The first is a light sleep, and we begin to drowse. Stage two is deeper, more relaxed; our eyes begin rolling slowly. We may twitch suddenly or awaken to a noise — and insist we haven't been asleep for the last ten minutes!

If undisturbed, we settle into stage three. We become very relaxed and breathe evenly and slowly. Temperature and blood pressure decline as heart rate slows — and we can sleep through a thunderstorm without awakening.

Then we sink into stage four, the deepest, most restful level: "The sleep of the weary," one researcher calls it. "Ordinarily a person devotes a large portion of his sleep time in the first half of the night to stage four."[3] This is the sleep we need in order to be restored and energized for the next day.

Insomnia

Most of us enjoy sleep time — except when we're fighting insomnia! Insomnia is the terrible hour or two you spend trying to *get* to sleep when you *must* sleep. You lie there thinking of tomorrow's work, which needs a rested mind and body; or you relive the frustrations and hurts of the day. That's insomnia, a curse for millions of people at some time.

Ten years ago Americans were spending over 100 million dollars a year for prescription sedatives — over 350 million dollars when over-the-counter drugs were included. That was before we moved into the Valium and Quaalude era. Since then the price tag for drug relaxation has multiplied in what some authorities are now calling an epidemic of drug dependency. Yet with all this chemical assistance, one still can't get a good night's sleep!

A proper diet is important. Overeating, using more salt and sugar than we need, snacking on junk food rather than eating lunch, and drinking too much caffeine throw our metabolism out of whack. Improper eating takes its toll in our sleep patterns.

A reasonable amount of exercise is necessary, too. A brisk mile walk every day would help us sleep. If, like me, you are chained to a desk all day, your body needs to exercise itself somehow. Some find a nighttime ritual helpful before getting in bed: a shower, brushing teeth, a little preparation for tomorrow. You can't just rush along at high speed, dive into bed, and expect to start "catching *Z's*," as they say.

Some people find that reading is helpful. Don't choose an exciting "whodunit," or you'll find yourself more awake than when you climbed into bed! Rather, read something meditative, something uplifting.

I'm also particular in choosing television programs. Many programs are too stimulating to watch just before bedtime. The hour or so before sleep is a time to wind down, not be wound up again.

Life is too short...

Change Our Focus

Many persons today complain of being stretched beyond their limits. The drive is always for *more*. And the enormous quantities of tranquilizers, muscle relaxers, sleeping pills, and alcohol used seem to affirm that we are in a crisis of overstimulation.

Yet the high-speed people on the go are still held up as models. Books and magazines try to let each of us into the secret of "reaching the top." Until we change the focus of our admiration, we're not apt to get any relief.

The focus of the problem is our failure to recognize what our great-grandparents lived by: nighttime is for sleeping. Our bodies have natural rhythms.

Are you an early-morning lark? Then late television is definitely not for you. Are you an all-night owl? Then you may need to rearrange your daytime schedule to provide the seven to nine hours of sleep most of us need for good mental and physical health. Our bodies have an established daily rhythm that is very difficult to change. In fact some authorities now question whether an individual's daily pattern can be changed.

Research shows that during the day, when most of us are at our best, our bodies go through a rhythmic rise and fall of energy levels, similar to the stages of sleep at night. The rise and fall of our energy levels seems to be a function of our central nervous system, controlled in the biochemical centers of the body. The twenty-four-hour rhythm is tied to the rhythm of day and night. And as experiments seem to show, we are not going to alter that rhythm without creating unpredictable difficult problems for our mental and physical welfare. Yet we like to try, don't we? We like to stretch day into night, cram seventy-two hours into a weekend.

Rather than riding roughshod over our inner clocks, we need to grow familiar with our own biological rhythms. We need to work when we're up and learn to ease up and relax

to miss a nap when we need one

every ninety minutes or so. A few minutes of deep relaxation at that point is far better than a cup of coffee and will increase the efficiency of the next hour or so.

Theresa is a junior executive in an advertising agency. She takes a brief rest in her chair nearly every hour. "I let myself relax. Let everything go out of my mind. I take the telephone off the hook so no call disturbs me. And I try to get down to the edge of sleep for a few minutes — that's all it needs, and I'm refreshed."[4]

It makes sense to admire a slower, more relaxed model — the woman achiever who is satisfied to set her own goal, the man who refuses to work a killing sixteen-hour day, the parent who says that sleeping is part of being a loving parent! We need to understand who we are and what our task is.

Instead of relying on sleeping pills, we *can* develop a healthier pattern of living that will allow us to enjoy natural sleep, to think with clarity, and to make our daily work a thanksgiving offering to God.

Chapter 4

Life is too short ...
to worry about gray hair
or wrinkles

"Mirrors don't lie," they say. Each year adds some sign of aging, some reminder of mortality. But each new year also opens new doors to new possibilities.

I'VE NEVER SEEN forty candles on a birthday cake. Maybe the cakes aren't big enough. Or maybe we don't want to count forty candles. Or maybe we don't want to be reminded of how many years have passed. But we're all on one side or the other of forty, and it's significant to think about mid-life.

This summer a friend of mine celebrated her fortieth birthday. Six of us took her out to dinner, and we celebrated. We celebrated the meaning of her life, celebrated the gift our friendship has been, and celebrated our faith in the tomorrows we look forward to.

Mid-Life Questions

Forty is usually the marker that brings to consciousness certain questions and emotions. Some people experience forty as a crisis. One friend described her feelings: "I was going along just fine, and I didn't expect my fortieth birthday to make any difference. But it did! It has! I don't feel like the same person I was last year!" Others take year forty with the assurance that changes are gradual and not much more critical than any other particular time.

Turning forty often activates some anxious thoughts and questions: "My life is now probably half-lived. I have time — yes — but my time has limits."

"What difference do I make?" is one way the mid-life question comes. "Does anyone need me anymore?" is another.

For emotional health, we must feel needed and useful, but the ways to achieve this are individual. Harry and John were friends and co-workers. They had joined a large company when they were both in their late twenties. Ten years later each had advanced to heading a department. As they came to mid-life Harry and John began to feel more pressured. The next advancements would take them into the vice-presidential group. John decided he didn't want to live the rest of his life in that kind of pressure; Harry decided to "go for it."

Both Harry and John were responding to the need to feel productive and useful — even though they chose two different roads.

At first John's decision to leave the company and choose a different profession seemed more difficult and upsetting. However ten years later it was apparent that John had made peace with himself and his abilities; his decision freed him to develop new strengths, and his later years were fulfilling.

And that is what mid-life is really about. It's a time to ask: What is most important in the remaining years? What do I want to give to family? What do I want to give to work, to profession, or to community? What do I want for myself?

Awareness of Limited Time

The fortieth birthday is different! I never expected to be forty! If you think you're alone with these feelings, take heart. You have more and more company.

Remember how Jack Benny spent *years* at thirty-nine? (I guess if you remember Jack Benny, you're telling something about your age!) But statistics tell us that not only am I personally growing older, but a higher percentage of the population is now forty or older.

Along with this advancing average age has come increasing interest in what happens at different stages of adult life. Why is the fortieth birthday significant?

In *Passages* Gail Sheehy showed mid-life as a turning point: "Deep down a change begins to register in the gut-level perceptions of safety and danger, time and no time, aliveness and stagnation, self and others."[1]

It's always easier to observe what is happening with others, isn't it. Our neighbor, Ron, owned a mechanic's garage. He opened at 6 A.M. and stayed opened until 11 P.M. The family never took more than two days off at a time; Ron didn't have time to go to church or to basketball games to watch his son play. Ron gave up many things because his work demanded so much time and energy.

But about the time Ron turned forty, his younger son got into trouble at school, and the family was recommended for counseling. Ron took off long enough to attend the sessions, too. About the same time, mid-life questions began to affect his values.

Five years later, Ron *looks* different. He has grown a beard, cut down his working hours, and developed an interest in antiques. Most important, he has become a friend to his son.

This new inner perception of "who he is" and "why he is here" and "what has meaning" is reflected in changes in appearance and lifestyle.

This awareness of limited time comes to the consciousness in different ways in different persons. Robert Raines was a minister who left the ministry to enter a writing and counseling profession in mid-life. Others in mid-life have left professions to enter the ministry.

One sharp reminder of the relentless passage of time comes as persons in mid-life look at their now-aged parents. Georgia's father had a stroke that affected his bodily functions, and so Georgia made an apartment in her house for her parents. "Watching my parents' helplessness forced me to ask questions about my own preparation for old age," Georgia told me.

Most persons in mid-life find they are increasingly involved again with parents. The effects of aging, of dependency, and of "aloneness" seem to focus more clearly. Mary talks about how hard it is to reverse roles with her mother. "I hadn't realized how subconsciously I'd counted on my mother being available when I *needed* her until now. Now I'm becoming a caregiver, and my mother is dependent on me. It is hard work taking care of my invalid mother, but the hardest part is the feelings about changing roles. I find myself asking again 'who am I?' I thought that was all over."

A fortieth birthday isn't really any different from the thirty-ninth or forty-first. But the changes that come in mid-life are real, and we need to move into those changes with faith and a sense of purpose. "Choosing life" is the challenge of each stage in development — including mid-life.

Meeting Mid-Life Crises

I've always loved the poetry of Robert Browning, and I'm appreciating more the insight:

> Grow old along with me!
> The best is yet to be,
> The last of life, for which the first was made:

Life is too short...

Our times are in His hand
Who saith "A whole I planned,
Youth shows but half; trust God:
see all, nor be afraid!"
(from "Rabbi Ben Ezra")

Why does mid-life look so scary? I think one reason is the strains we've observed in many marriages. Men and women seem to experience mid-life questions at different times. And since their life-experience is different in the first half of life, the second half will also be different.

For instance Keith is beginning to say to himself: "My family is growing up, and I hardly know them. I've been putting in too many hours at work. I want more quiet evenings at home and with my family. I want to do things with my son and wife."

Keith's wife is feeling, "Now that my children take less of my time and energy, I'm ready to look for a job outside the home. I want to test my skills in the job market and see what I can do."

It's easy to see why Keith and his wife face a crisis. New schedules, new priorities for housework, new budgets, new commitments to community and church life, new relationships to family members — all come with mid-life changes, and changes are stressful. It is no wonder that divorce is increasing among the couples who are between forty and forty-five. But divorce does not solve the problems for most persons.

Ida looks back from the perspective of five years and says that the problems she thought were her husband's were really her own. She still had to deal with her insecurity and anger and feelings of being used. She still had to face her own need to make life meaningful. The divorce she wanted so badly at the time only postponed her work and made it harder and lonelier.

What are the resources available to help those who feel the ground shaking under them at age forty? One source of help is in books. Our circumstances will not be the same as those of the author, but we can learn from the insights and responses of others, especially those who have made an extensive study of the mid-life period.

Another source of help may be friends. Usually they are experiencing some of the same questions. When we are open enough to voice our own needs, we give others the freedom to say, "Yes, I'm feeling like that too." And it helps to know that we are not alone.

Another source of help that many are reluctant to try is counselors — those trained to help focus our questions and help us make wiser choices. I believe that God speaks to us with care and guidance through the voices of many helpers.

For some, mid-life does bring crisis. Others struggle with questions without much outer sign of turbulence. For each one, the goal is to move from the questions to satisfying and meaningful answers, from the breaking apart to the reassembling of the self. This is to say — to move on toward maturity and wholeness.

Perhaps birthday cakes aren't big enough for forty candles, but life is too good to quit celebrating. The new perceptions that life has limits, that our own life will someday end, will spur new growth in us if we don't retreat in fear. I think forty candles may look much better than thirty-nine.

Nurturing Others

Chapter 5

*L*ife is too short ...
to not spend time with our parents

After giving to us so much, they ask so little: a weekly letter,
phone calls, staying in touch! Then comes a time when they need
help to maintain a home, or even full-time care.

WHAT DO WE *OWE* OUR PARENTS? Let's start with one
fact: We owe them our lives — we certainly wouldn't be here if
our parents hadn't conceived us. But I'm uncomfortable with
the word *owe*. I'd like to think that love more than meets all that
is owed between parent and child.

I think we owe our parents respect — the respect of
human dignity. We also owe it to them to keep in touch, to
include them in our lives, and to allow them to enjoy the love of
their grandchildren. I think we owe them the attention and
encouragement that allows them to live independently as long
as they can. And, of course, we owe our parents adequate care
when they become dependent.

Respect for Parents

Respecting parents as individuals — what does that mean? I have to think of Tina, a six year old with all the energy she gets from eating good food and being young. She dances, she jumps, she runs, and she hardly ever stops to talk. But her grandpa has some hearing loss. Tina wanted to tell Grandpa about her new friend at school, but she kept bouncing around as she talked, and he didn't hear her. "Tina, stop jumping and go up to Grandpa so he'll know you are talking to him," her mother suggested. Tina stopped long enough to talk to her grandfather.

Hearing is more difficult for many older people, but the extra effort to come closer, to speak more distinctly, is a way of respecting them. And don't forget to listen! Listen to their wisdom earned in years of living. Listen to their stories of the past. Listen to their wishes for today.

Talking together, respecting their individuality, honoring their preferences where we can, loving the best in each of them — I do owe my parents this respect. They *are* special persons.

Loving Relationships

In a questionnaire given to men and women over sixty-five, the overwhelming response was "we want to be *needed* and to feel self-esteem." We owe our parents continuing inclusion in family — in loving relationships — as much as *we* and *they* are able.

Special family celebrations are times to include parents and grandparents. They enjoy being part of the birthdays, graduation parties, bridal showers, and holiday dinners. Grandparents also enjoy quiet times with one or two grandchildren. Reading together, teaching a young one to knit, helping to build sand castles, or fixing a broken tricycle — all make special ties between young and old.

Life is too short...

We have to be realistic. Some parents and children never did get along well together. It's unrealistic to expect all the hurts to be healed, the broken communication to be restored, or the painful personality traits to disappear by the magic of aging. Yet we do owe our parents whatever relationships we can maintain. We may find the relationships to hold new delights and rewarding years together.

Including parents in your family may or may not mean having them live in your home. Most parents are better off living independently. *But* if there comes a time when you believe it would be better for you and your parents to live in the same house, don't expect that your love will make every day smooth. Living together always requires give and take, talking it over, and sometimes an explosion. Three generations in one house can line up "two against one" — and that hurts.

The more the aged can be involved in helping and in feeling useful, the better they'll feel about themselves.

Meeting Material Needs

Many old people do *not* have adequate physical care. According to government statistics nearly one-fourth of the elderly in the United States today live *below* the poverty level. Yet it can be difficult for struggling young families to provide their parents with the necessities of life.

Charlie's parents lived in the old house in the country where they had lived while he was growing up, but Charlie didn't get back there very often and gradually drifted out of touch with his parents. Working in a machine shop, keeping food on the table for four growing sons, making mortgage and car payments, and paying dental and medical bills kept Charlie busy. "I figured they were getting along all right. They'd call if they needed help," he said. Charlie forgot that as his parents aged, their house was also getting older. They couldn't keep up with the repairs. Since his visits were hurried and months apart, his parents assumed he didn't need to hear about their problems! But one day Charlie got a call from the hospital where his mother was being treated for exposure and malnutrition. Charlie was appalled; he'd had no idea how bad off they were!

If we don't remain close to our parents, we *won't* know their needs. And we won't learn about them by rushing in with a breathless "How are you? I'm on my way to pick up Johnny and I just have a minute or two!"

Life is too short not to care for our parents. It was while watching his mother prepare a small lunch that Earl saw a kitchen faucet dripping and a stove burner that didn't work. So he fixed them. "Caring" always takes some time. And if we live far apart, we'll need to budget for visits and long-distance calls.

Dealing with Aging

Parents, whether they are twenty, forty, or eighty, are always "old" to their children! But there comes a time when aging parents need certain assistance. What do we owe our parents as they lose the ability to earn a living and to care for all their own needs?

"Studies show that those [older persons] who stay in their own homes are healthier and happier than those who give up and let a son or daughter take care of them."[1] Familiar things, freedom to plan their own lives, access to work or crafts they enjoy, some sense of usefulness — all these challenge the elderly to use their minds and bodies.

When my parents first retired from the farm, they considered moving to a small apartment. Instead they found a smaller home. It's large enough for their crafts and the gardening they still love. My father took a part-time job nearby. With just a little help on upkeep, they are enjoying happy, independent years there.

Sometimes the death of one spouse forces a decision. Shall mother or father move in with one family, or shall the children help that mother or father to live alone? There are many alternatives to consider. One might hire someone to live with the parent or to take in a meal each day. One could hire part-time nursing care or find a residence unit with central dining room. One solution doesn't fit all families.

Lois and her family did choose to have her mother move in with them. "We talked it over and made the choice as a family," Lois said. "And our decision included the fact that our children were all going to school, and they wanted grandmother to come. Also my mother was still active, able to care for herself. I could continue my part-time work in nursing, and I knew that would help keep my perspective healthy."

As Lois's mother became more unsteady on her feet, they hired someone to stay with Mother while Lois worked. Finally her mother lost all mobility and required full-time nursing care, so they decided on a nursing home.

Lois's mother knew that she was loved, cared for, and included in the family. She could trust their care even when the last, hard decision came.

When Relating Is Difficult

We must also say that there are some things we do *not* owe our parents. One woman, Liza, told me with shaking hands of how her family with two teenagers was being torn apart by the mean-spirited manipulation of her mother-in-law who had moved into her home. Liza was just "getting through" her days and nights with the help of drugs the doctor prescribed. She saw no alternatives but the breakup of her family and her own collapse. Now we do *not* owe broken health or a broken home to our parents. There *are* alternatives. It's important to sort out the strands in any difficult problem.

Each of us is different and our circumstances vary. Florence was able to take care of her mother in her home for the last two years of her mother's life. "And I have no regrets," Florence said.

Sue took care of her father in her home, too. "But he was

a bitter and mean person all of his life, and he was that way when he was ninety! We had ten very hard years!"

Perhaps most typical was Lulu: "I took my father in while he could still be some help. And we had our good times and our bad times! But I'm not sorry. You just have to have a lot of patience because you don't know all the pain they're feeling and what it's like to be where they are."

"Life is too short not to write regularly to your parents," my friend said. I like to think that writing, visiting, phoning, and exchanging gifts are all extensions of the loving relationship that shaped us. The parent-child relationship is active and dynamic. But as the years pass, our roles subtly change. Needs and dependencies shift and personalities emerge in surprising configurations. The caregiver eventually becomes the one in need of care; the one who supported grows frail. This is the opportunity for love to rejoice in giving, to be patient and kind, and to empathize with weakness and loss. Life is too short not to love our parents, and, of course, not to teach our children how to love theirs.

Life is too short...

Chapter 6

Life is too short ...
to let a good marriage die

A group of men were asked how they would choose between "A congenial job and an unhappy home," or "a happy home and an uncongenial job." They voted, "give me a happy home; I'll put up with the job!"

BACK IN THE 1600s someone said, "Marriage is a desperate thing!" Some things haven't changed since then. Many married people end up agreeing with the sentiment.

Facing the challenges of the *middle years* of marriage has been compared to the season of autumn or crossing the Rocky Mountains or a crucible. In other words, the middle years of marriage are a testing time.

Psychologists describe mid-life marriage as a time of radical questioning. Questions arise about career and lifestyle, about religious convictions and one's contribution to the community or the world, about one's sense of self-worth and basic commitments to family. And, inevitably, marriage is affected by this unrest and shifting direction.

Change Brings Fear

David Thomas is a marriage counselor who identifies *four fears* that are common to mid-life marriage. He says that during this time, partners fear the "gap" that has grown between them. They fear the limitations of mid-life as well as the limitations of the future. Another fear comes from facing one's self and taking full responsibility for one's actions. And finally, he thinks many people fear that they are "odd" or "too different" or even "sick." Is it really normal to have these fears at mid-life?[1]

My own experiences and what I've observed from friends all say that these fears *are* normal. Fear always comes with change. Change is a risk. But you can't stay with the past, and you wouldn't want to.

If you have been married for fifteen to twenty-five years, you've had time to grow in different directions. One partner in the marriage has probably developed expertise in some profession, made friends related to that work, perhaps even learned a language only the "in" people use. Very seldom do married partners become experts in the same field. So a gap develops.

Through the years spouses develop different hobbies and ways of relaxing. They develop different expectations of their children. Partners often develop different spiritual disciplines. Or one partner becomes active in church life while the other just "attends."

I could list many ways in which gaps develop between a husband and wife during twenty years of marriage. And I *don't* want to imply that this is unhealthy or bad. Rather differences probably offer a good basis for a solid marriage in the later years. You can share across a gap; you can build bridges.

How are bridges built? One man told me that he and his wife were finding it difficult to "stretch" to meet each other. They decided that one bridge they needed to build was simply spending a regular bit of time together.

Another couple I know chose to begin refinishing furniture together; that grew into a shared job after about five years.

One thing I've observed is that two people do not make a lot of new connections at one time. Bridges are built by symbols of caring — choosing to reach toward each other, beginning a regular activity together. As couples work at their relationship in one area — perhaps sharing a hobby — the difference in feelings about each other diffuses through other areas, including the sexual.

Marriage is not static, and the middle years may be either a challenge to grow or a gap that widens until the partnership breaks.

A Dictionary of Divorce

A magazine article tells the story of Thomas and Marjorie who were divorced after more than thirty years of marriage. Thomas had loved his wife. Their friends had called the marriage "perfect" and were shocked at the news of the breakup. The aloneness after the separation was so painful that he wondered if he could make it alone, but he couldn't live *with* her either. The accusations and the language of hatred they had learned to use in thirty years were too devastating.

When a husband or wife begins to accuse the other, a history of togetherness is broken. Thomas said, "Think of all the things one can accuse the other of: working too late . . . never taking you to lunch . . . never taking a vacation . . . never sending flowers . . . not telling the truth. The list is very long." And, of course, either husband or wife can accuse the other of having an affair. Thomas says that "once the accusations start, the language of divorce is set in motion and only rarely can it be stopped."

Thomas included several other phrases that belong in his dictionary of divorce: "That's not so at all. That's not what you meant! You don't know what you're talking about. . . . No, I don't want to go for a walk! Do you have to mess up the sink every time you use it? Why do you always ignore me when we're out? Look at all the sacrifices I've made for you all these years!"[2]

Let's think of words that build trust rather than destroy — words that say, "I'd like to know what you meant," or "I'd like to help you with raking the lawn," or "I disagree with you on this, can we talk more about it?" Let's use words that express patience, generosity, forgiveness, and acceptance as we talk with our partner.

How many ways can you think of saying, "I want to grow, and I want to give you room to grow, and I think we can support each other"? That's a relationship of partners rather than adversaries!

Achieving a successful, long-lasting marriage is like scaling a mountain: it takes hard work.

As I look around me I see two basic approaches: One says, "I'm changing; I have to find a new lifestyle, and my husband (or wife) no longer fits me. I'll begin again to see what I can do." So the marriage is dissolved and both partners begin the process of salvaging pieces from the ruins. The other approach says, "My wife (or husband) and I have grown apart; we'll have to work at new understanding and maybe make a new schedule to talk about changes we'd both like." The years of change may be difficult, but the rewards include knowing that you have loved wisely, that "love begets love," and that you are committed to the high vows you both made.

Mutuality

This summer I attended the wedding of one of my daughter's friends. Near the end of a beautiful ceremony, the bride and groom stepped up to a small table with three candles: two small candles lit on either side of one large candle. The bride and groom each picked up one of the small candles and together lit the single, large candle. Then they blew out the

Life is too short...

small candles they were holding. I think I understood the symbolism: one large, single, unified light. But why blow out the small candles? Two people should not snuff out their individuality when they marry.

I'm sure my daughter's friends quickly learned that two individual candles were still burning. It takes work and time — and probably relighting — to keep the candle of unity burning. A marriage needs individual lights as the source of the light of unity.

I know of one marriage in which the wife feels as if her candle has been smothered — squashed out by the icy flame of a husband whose single ambition has been to become a millionaire. Now that their children have left home, she doesn't know if she can live with that iciness. She wonders if she has any capacity for love or light left.

On the other hand, I know of marriages that seem to find ways of relighting the candles, sometimes for each other, sometimes by relighting one small candle from the unity candle of the marriage.

The candles are only symbols, and what really matters in a Christian marriage is that there is both *permanence* and *mutuality.* Neither is adequate without the other.

Middle age seems to be a time to readjust the "mutuality." Is one partner overburdened with financial worries? Is one given all the responsibility for loving? Is one always strong and the other dependent? Is one expected to make all necessary changes to please the other?

In *Meet Me in the Middle* Charlotte Holt Clinebell writes about how a marriage can change. She found that when only one partner wants change, that person can bring *some* gradual change. She says that change always has the possibility of making a marriage better — or worse.[3]

The commitment I made to my partner was to love through all the hard times as well as the good times of life. I also made a commitment to love the person he would become.

He made the same commitment to me. We've passed our twenty-fifth anniversary, so we know the tugs and pulls toward separateness that are so strong during the years of raising a family.

I will always see my husband's decision to move from New York to Virginia for my job opportunity as an expression of his commitment. The job I was offered in radio and writing was an opportunity for personal development that was so exciting I hardly dared to hope. And my husband's enthusiastic response was equally as exciting. "Of course I'll move for this position you've been offered," Don said. "I can find accounting positions in any area of the country." Our children were at transition points in their school life, and so we moved our family.

We chose to strengthen our marriage in that move, and we have had to continue to make choices that bridge our differences. I know that others (for whatever reason) cannot rebuild a marriage, and so divorce one another. But I believe that a good marriage is worth the commitment to change, to mutuality, and to growth; it is worth the risk of pain, the demands of reconciliation, and the patience of love.

Chapter 7

Life is too short ...
to let a day pass without hugging
each of our children

"Four hugs a day helps keep the doctor away," according to one authority. Our need to be touched and hugged is as basic as our need for food. Babies do not thrive without cuddling. And evidence abounds that hugging is a powerful way to help a child, teen or adult — to say nothing of oneself — feel wonderful!

WHEN I CLOSED THE DOOR behind me I felt as if my spirit had been shredded. I didn't know where I would find the strength to go back to work one more day. My head ached and the tears came. My little daughter had heard me come in and she met me in the kitchen.

"Mom, what's wrong?" she asked as she hugged my arm. We sat down together and she hugged me again and again. Slowly the aches inside me subsided and I felt able to face at least the next hour.

"Life is too short to let a day pass without hugging your spouse and each of your children!" The meaning of hugging is beyond what words can capture — and that's exactly why it's so wonderful.

Nothing works as well as a hug to express empathy for a fielding error that lost a game or for the person whose friend is choosing another friend. A hug is an appropriate expression of respect for your teenager who has just added another inch in height. Hugs and laughs can turn frustrations into shared memories. Hugs are greetings as well as goodbyes. A hug symbolizes the commitment to care for each other, which is the central meaning of family. But of course it takes more than hugging to build family relationships that are healthy and joyful.

Toni Bosco, a mother of six, an author and teacher, says that she thinks of a healthy family as "whole." And the whole family is one "where there is a sense of unity and peace; where all the members of the family feel comfortable; where they care for each other, stick up for each other and would never deliberately hurt one another."[1]

Few of us recall our growing-up years as times when relationships were always peaceful; few of us would claim that our families now always experience wholeness. But this sense of unity, of caring for and trusting one another, of becoming "whole" is our goal in family living. And I believe that family wholeness involves a commitment to good parenting.

Parents Are Models

In the great surge toward self-expression and individual freedom, many have relegated parenting to a low priority. But if a family is to achieve a sense of caring and belonging — each member feeling *loved* and learning to *love* — then parents must accept responsibility.

Mother *and* father (or mother *or* father in single-parent families) must give energy and commitment to this task of raising a family. Good parenting begins with *who* we are. The strongest instinct of each child is to imitate father and mother.

Recently I shared a seat on a bus with a girl I think was about ten years old. She and her brother were returning home, where they lived with their father, after spending a weekend with their mother. "I want to be just like my mother when I grow up," she said. "My mother is a legal secretary, and she's always completely organized. When we get to her house, she says, 'We'll have dinner tonight at 6:30, and then we'll go to a movie. Tomorrow we'll do this and this and this!' She lets us know exactly what's expected of us and when."

The ten year old went on to tell me how she plans her own daily schedules ("like my mother does") and where she is planning to go to college ("where my mother went because I'm going to be a legal secretary like her!").

Many parents are concerned about having authority in the home and in the lives of their children. Some set up an artificial structure with strict rules, not realizing that their true authority is the way their children perceive them. Most children do not imitate one parent as specifically as my ten-year-old seatmate, but children do respond to the real authority of who their parents are. If we'd had more time together, I'm sure that I'd have learned that this girl is learning to like the same kind of friends her mother has and looks at life from the same perspective. She *trusts* her mother.

Trust Is Basic to Family

Trust is the basis for healthy family relationships. Trust is the assurance a child has that he or she can depend on the parent. It begins with the baby's first cry and the parents' response. Time after time, one experience after another, teaches a child that parents can or cannot be trusted. When mother or father says "no," trust is the assurance that it is in the child's interest.

Trust is the mutual, growing sense of connection. Trust is the basis for the first steps toward separation and independence. Trust will finally maintain the relationship between parent and adult offspring.

Trust is very fragile. Sometimes one broken promise undermines trust, but children also learn to forgive — if their parents forgive each other and their children. Here's one place that energy and commitment to parenting are tested. A promise to picnic on Saturday sounds like fun on Wednesday. But Saturday morning, sleeping in or finishing the cleaning or mowing the lawn, moves that picnic down on your list of priorities. Parents must balance priorities of work with the priorities of relationship. And when parents fail, they should acknowledge the failure and seek forgiveness.

When Debbie comes home with a note from the teacher asking her parents to come in for a conference, can she count on her parents' love and support, even while they hear about the trouble she's in? Love cannot be conditional, offered only when a child pleases parents. That's not love, and a child can't depend on that.

Teenage runaways are one evidence that many families have not built trust between parents and children. When the teen gets into trouble, it is easier to run away if love has been granted only for "being good." Years of cumulative experiences either pull adolescents toward reconciliation or convince them that there is no hope.

"Trust is knowing that a promise will not be broken; an assurance that you will never turn your back and walk away from the person you claim to love; trust is the confidence that your love is unconditional, not subject to ifs, buts, or exceptions."[2]

Trust is the first step in a child's response to God. Parents cannot give their child *faith*, but parents can be *trustworthy*.

Love Is Active

If you were to choose a single word to describe your family's interaction, it would probably be "love." The question is, how does love act? One father said, "Jamie knows I love him. But I'm just too busy to play with him." Jamie's mother added, "Or to work with him."

Life is too short...

Parents can *say* they love (and sometimes parents even have difficulty *saying,* "I love you"), but the proof is always in how they act. Parents must spend time with their children, to talk together, to work and play together, to learn together.

One interesting study was made on the importance of father-child interaction. Taking third-grade boys, the researcher divided them into four groups: those whose father was absent before the child was five, those whose father left after they were five, those whose father was present but spent less than six hours per week with them, and those with high father-presence — more than two hours a day of father-child interaction.

The researcher found that the high father-presence — the group whose fathers spend more than two hours a day interacting — achieved significantly better in academic performance, and their whole outlook on life was better.[3]

A little boy watched his father polishing the car. "Hey, Dad, your car's worth a lot, isn't it?" he asked.

"Yes," his Dad replied, "it cost a lot of money. It pays to take good care of it. When I trade the car in, it will be worth more if I've taken good care of it."

After some silence the son said, "Dad, I guess I'm not worth very much, am I?"[4]

Parents need not give up in discouragement if their time with family is *necessarily* limited by work or by the fact that one is parenting alone. Learn to make the *minutes* together count. If children must take on extra chores to help, working together can be quality time.

After a divorce, one young mother had to go to work to support herself and her four-year-old daughter. She found a nursery school for her little girl, but both of them missed their days at home together. The child scowled at her mother every day when she picked her up at nursery school. One day the little girl refused to go with her. "You're not my mommy," she said. "You're just the lady who goes to work."

Instead of responding with guilt or defensiveness, the young mother answered, "No, I'm the mommy who *comes home* from work because I love you."[5]

The one rule I know to help us understand how love *acts* is the one Jesus gave: "Do to others what you would like them to do to you"(Matt. 7:12). This rule of love reminds me to be sensitive to my children's feelings: how do I feel when I am put on the spot or accused unfairly? When I work hard and my effort is dismissed with criticism? When I'm ignored or my ideas are sarcastically belittled?

What makes me feel like trying again? What makes me feel loved?

The children we are parenting are *persons*. The child's *feelings* respond just as yours and mine. Stopping to ask, "How would *I* want to be treated," reminds me to extend second or third or fourth chances. It inspires me to listen respectfully, to praise generously, to cry with the hurts as well as laugh with the joys.

A Hug Feels Good

"How important is it for people to show their love?" a group of fifth-grade children were asked. A little boy said, "I like to come home every day because my mom hugs me and gives me a glass of milk." A girl said, "Love should show itself in kindness, consideration, and unselfishness. When I feel loved, I feel secure, and I feel safe."

I like the idea of "wholeness" as an antidote to the pet theories or current fads about discipline and "how-to-parent-in-x-number-of-lessons." Parenting is not a formula so much as a creative discipline to teach loving. Parenting is not a license for total control but the responsibility to lead and guide toward maturity. To quote Toni Bosco again: "Good parenting is our contribution to the continuation of life itself, and it is only love that makes sense out of our lives."[6]

"Wholeness" is a family goal that is both individual and

collective for both parents and children. A sense of unity, based on trust and love, will not shred with the tensions and conflicts in a family, but it will provide the basis for mutually supportive relationships through the hard times and the easier time.

Chapter 8

Life is too short ...
to keep all our floors shiny

Television portrays women in a way that would have us believe that they can find ultimate satisfaction and meaning in life by gazing into mirrored reflections in sterile tile floors, ceramic sinks, and streakfree glass doors. But floors and sinks and glass doors can be spotless only if they are unused, and unused, they are worthless. Floors are to walk on; sinks are to wash in; and doors are to keep friends in and foes out.

"YOU'RE RIGHT! You're going to be a mother." The doctor's smile confirmed my own diagnosis of the changes I was feeling. From now on I would be a mother. I would care for an infant, then a toddler, a child, an adolescent, a teenager, an adult. I knew that my life would change, but I failed to realize how completely.

I soon realized how completely this tiny new bundle had changed both my priorities and values. During my child's first months of infancy I learned that feeding the baby is more important than any other routine. A child's cry in the night awakens even the heaviest sleeper. And suddenly, inexplicably, the first smile, first tooth, first step, first words became more exciting than a salary hike (even though they were equally welcome).

My image of "house beautiful" was totally renovated. Bassinets, high chairs, and diaper pails do not match many decors, and mine was no exception. But we welcomed the variation. During the toddler stage we moved plants and all breakables out of reach. But where can you move the kitchen floor? Cleaning the floor was the same as inviting tracks of mud, but I finally learned I didn't want it any other way. Every passing year deepened my realization that our home was for us, for our use.

I like the way Cecil Myers describes home's meaning: "Home is the beginning point of everything. Here life makes up its mind. It is not just the beginning place of biological life, but of moral, ethical, mental, spiritual, and emotional life as well. Parents have the very first chance to affect the feelings, the beliefs, the ideas of the child."[1]

Instead of seeing my home as a showplace, I see it as the place to nurture people — parents as well as children. At home we learn who we are and what we can do — that's self-image — and whether or not we are loveable — that's self-acceptance. At home we learn how to forgive, how to express love, and what to do when we are hurt. We develop attitudes toward work, and toward how we use time, energy, and money. We learn prejudices about people and viewpoints about our world. We learn that the world is a safe and friendly place or a frightening and hostile environment.

Love and Forgiveness are Learned at Home

Back in the 1800s, the French writer Victor Hugo wrote: "The supreme happiness in life is the conviction that we are loved." That conviction is learned at home. Infants learn that being loved means being fed when hungry, changed when wet, and cuddled when uncomfortable. Children learn that being loved means being talked to, included in family plans, listened to, and receiving attention when hurt. There is an element of mystery in love — more than we can define or explain. Children learn that love is what we do as well as what we say.

Forgiving is best learned at home. My friend Vel says that she thinks of a family as a place for second chances — a place to begin again. She tells about two days when she was working very hard on one of her projects. During that time all three of her sons told her she was a grouch. "Finally I had to take time to listen to them. And I had to ask their forgiveness for harsh and cutting things I had said to them."

Some parents think asking forgiveness of their children is a sign of weakness, an undermining of authority, but I believe the opposite is true.

In a recent conversation with my daughter I was telling her about my father's life, the hardships he had faced and how they had affected the way he parented me. One of the times I remember most clearly, I told her, was the time he asked me to forgive him. I was only about seven years old, but I still remember it vividly. He had been plowing and I interrupted him, which made him very angry. He threatened to throw a stone at me if I didn't get out of there. I turned for the house, crying. That evening he asked me to come outside to talk, and then he told me he was sorry. He asked me to forgive him.

When I finished my story she looked at me with tears in her eyes. "You know," she said, "one of the times I remember most vividly with Dad is when he asked me to forgive him."

I'm convinced that homes should be places where we learn to forgive each other, and we can only learn by being forgiven. "Families are people admitting their poverty of spirit . . . forgiving easily, seasoning the rough spots with a bit of humor and accepting each other in spite of imperfections."[2]

Work Habits are Learned at Home

I can clearly remember one story my father told us about the little boy who got tired of planting corn. On a hot summer afternoon, he wanted to go swimming, so he just planted all the remaining seeds at the end of one row. Then he told his father he had finished planting the corn, and he ran off to enjoy a swim. I was horrified at such stupidity. "What happened when the corn plants came up?" I asked in alarm. My father's answer was the reminder I needed to establish good work habits of my own.

My mother also told a story about work habits. The main character in hers was a girl who swept dirt under the rug — until she was found out. There's probably a good reason I remember that story!

Those stories were told to teach us that work should be done conscientiously, done right, even if it meant taking a little more time. Mark says he was taught to work to get the job accomplished. All the joy was in being finished. In Cheri's home she learned to enjoy the *work* — just for the fun of working.

The world has room for all kinds of workers. Some work quickly, others meticulously. Some paint with bold, bright strokes; others fill every corner with fine detail. Some find all their definition of self in work; others work only to earn a living. Those who learn to do only what is required — who never give a little *more* — miss the *satisfaction* of work.

Carl works on an assembly line in a furniture factory, and he's often frustrated. Sometimes the furniture pieces come to him with hinges placed so carelessly that the doors won't close. "Some just don't take pride in their *work*," he says. Even in the most routine jobs, we can find ways to express our values.

Attitudes are Learned at Home

Happiness is an attitude learned at home. When the skies are threatening to rain on your parade, what do you do? Take

Life is too short...

an umbrella? Decide to stay home and have fun? Do you plan together or does the angriest member decide?

I was surprised to read recently that children of parents who are depressed learn to act depressed, and children of cheerful and optimistic parents learn cheerfulness and optimism. I had presumed that depression and cheerfulness were responses to life's situations, but one psychologist found evidence that even these attitudes are learned at home.

If we complain about what others "do to us" and do nothing to help ourselves, our children will learn to feel helpless. If we're honest about our feelings — our anger, hurt, frustration, and envy as well as joy, satisfaction, and love — our children will learn to accept their feelings and respond appropriately.

Sometimes my children helped me stay in touch with my feelings and attitudes. One time while standing beside me in the kitchen, my daughter Mary asked why I was angry.

"I'm not angry," I said. "What makes you think I'm angry?"

"Your voice is angry." But she said it with a hug.

I stopped and took inventory of what had happened and why I was angry. When I decided what I could do about the problem, my voice lost its angry tone.

Prejudices Are Learned at Home

Those who have researched attitudes say that *prejudice* is always learned. And it takes a few years to learn. Many children play happily together and are best friends with neighborhood children of other races — until they are *taught* to hate because of color.

Do you remember these words of the song from *South Pacific*? "You have to be taught to learn to hate. You have to be taught before it's too late. You have to be carefully taught."

Since prejudice has been learned over generations, ingrained in attitudes and expectations, it will take conscious effort for parents *not* to teach their children old fears and habits.

It is not only against persons of other races that we have prejudices. Those who choose a different faith, another type of government, or a different way of life arouse our fears. Can we live together? Is there room in the world for those who choose to be different from me?

The challenge is to make our homes a safe environment where we can nurture one another and develop emotionally healthy family members who are loving, forgiving, energetic, and accepting. These attitudes flourish without regard for shiny floors.

Life is too short...

Chapter 9

Life is too short ...
to let conflicts go unresolved

"You make me angry, you with your meek and mousey ways. You back into a corner and whimper. I dare you to come out and face me!" This is a challenge to learn how to resolve conflicts, a challenge to learn to win — sometimes.

I'M SURPRISED AT HOW MUCH conflict a little thing like a car can stir up. Our family was trying to cut down on our expenses by having only one car, which seemed reasonable enough to me. Lots of people do it. But there are five of us who spend our days in five different places. Believe me, it's amazing how important a car is. And I'm learning that it's not *only* transportation — a car is a symbol of status and independence. At least, that's what I've concluded as I've heard the arguments and angry accusations.

Conflict — A Part of Life

What do we expect to happen when we quarrel or fight? Obviously we want changes — something new and better, some results. If we didn't feel a deep demand for something better, we wouldn't be incited to fight for what we want. And what does the other person want? Sometimes the same thing; more often just the opposite.

Elementary! When we watch two people fighting, we can see it. When we're in the middle ourselves, it is not so clear — especially if we try to look at the feelings behind "needing the car today," for instance.

I grew up in a home where we were taught that fighting is always wrong, that we shouldn't claim our own rights, and that it was better to give in than to fight. Not that we always *followed* that, but we felt guilty about all our arguments or quarrels. And we never learned to communicate. We never learned to "fight fair."

If you have the same background, then we share a slow process of changing: confronting rather than running away from conflict, identifying and accepting our real feelings. Or you may find yourself on the other end — often confronting, often fighting, but not knowing how to repair the damage. You may feel that you never *really* win what you want most — love and concern for each other.

Conflict is a very natural part of our lives, and it can crop up in any relationship. In some periods we experience a great deal of conflict; at other times a relationship is easy and comfortable.

For those who have been living with severe conflicts for a long period of time, professional help is probably the best procedure. Most communities have some type of family counseling service that can help such individuals to find ways of dealing with the conflicts they are facing.

But for the occasional conflicts of daily living that most of us face at one time or another, simply learning the methods for resolving our differences may be all that's needed. We should not allow ourselves to flounder in a conflict situation when there are positive steps that can be taken toward resolution.

Life is too short...

Conflict Styles

In *When You Don't Agree* James Fairfield says there are five different conflict styles.[1] We generally follow one or two of these styles in all of our conflicts. These patterns range from "must win" to withdrawing, then trying compromise, sometimes giving in, but most ideally — resolving. Fairfield gives some new insight into how we can find resolution that moves toward an "I win *and* you win" pattern. This is another way of saying that even through conflict we can build a real base for love and have an environment in which love will flourish.

Fighting. One of the styles of conflict Fairfield lists is "I fight to win!" I think this style is one parents may find themselves using with their children. Also those who place a high priority on being *right* find themselves pushed into the "must win" style. Or a person who feels very unsure of himself or herself may compensate by having to "win" in every argument.

Withdrawing. A second way of handling conflict is withdrawing. Perhaps as children living with parents who practiced always winning, we learned to give up — to withdraw. We can withdraw physically: refuse to associate with some persons, limit where we go and with whom, move to another community, find another job, get a divorce. We can also withdraw psychologically: refuse to share any problems, refuse to look at any issues, refuse to acknowledge any conflicts. "Clamming up" is another way of describing this.

Neither of these two conflict-handling methods — "must win" or withdrawing — is effective if we are really interested in building a relationship. No one wants to be the losing partner in a relationship where one must always win. And a relationship can only die when one member chooses to withdraw rather than to resolve differences.

Compromising. A third pattern, which Fairfield terms compromise, offers more possibilities. "Give a little to win a little," or "give in this time to win next time." Perhaps a wife will compromise her personal goal of finishing college now to help her husband finish his education first. Then the plan is that he will help her work for her degree.

Yielding. A fourth possible reaction is yielding — "giving up this time" if we feel the relationship cannot stand a confrontation right now. Or maybe we give in when our position dictates it; we give in when the boss says so. Recently I read that a large percentage of women who work outside the home have had to put up with sexual innuendos from their bosses for many years. They felt they had no alternative. They were afraid of being given a low job rating or of losing their job. If you are caught in a conflict of authority like that, "giving in" is certainly the easiest — unless you consider the tension and frustration and possible ulcers that can follow.

Resolving. Ideally we want to resolve conflict — find ways of resolving differences so that both sides win! In *When You Don't Agree* James Fairfield tells one story that beautifully illustrates this possibility:

> Golda's mother-in-law loved to give her grandchildren expensive gifts. Some of the gifts Golda felt were not good for her children, and her resentment deepened with each present — whether the gift was appropriate or not. Golda's frustration grew and she realized that to go on without doing something about it could only lead to a breakdown in her family relationships.
>
> So the next time she visited with her mother-in-law, Golda opened the subject. "It took all my courage — and all the love I really have for her.
>
> "She was angry at first — but then she began to see that I wasn't rejecting her, and that I really had a point about spoiling the children."
>
> Golda and her mother-in-law negotiated a new arrangement. Now she brings smaller gifts of fruit the children like, and clothing they need. They *resolved* a

78   *Life is too short...*

situation that threatened their relationship, and both are achieving their personal goals.[2]

Causes of Conflict

It is said that "keeping peace in a large family requires patience, love, understanding — and at least two television sets!"

Family tensions and conflicts are natural when you have four different people with four different needs. You hardly have time to do fun things together, let alone sit down, discuss, and work through conflicts. Too often the conflicts get shoved aside; they seem to be forgotten, but they silently boil inside.

Beyond the tension of daily routines, crises occur simply because of the ongoing process of life. One family therapist lists ten basic crises that occur in most families: they move from the crisis of pregnancy, to having a second child, to first school experiences, the teen years, children leaving home and becoming parents themselves. Any of these items can cause major conflicts in the home.[3]

In an interview, James Fairfield stated that there are two main causes of conflict — lack of understanding and lack of communication. He gave the example of a husband who is mad at his wife, but he doesn't tell her what's wrong — he just broods. She can sense his anger but can only guess at the cause. Finally she can't take it anymore and asks what's wrong. Only when the tensions are brought into the open and honestly admitted can healing begin.

"That's only one illustration of how we bury our feelings and build conflict," Fairfield says. "We blame others for our anger instead of recognizing we make ourselves angry. And then we communicate all the wrong signals instead of resolving our conflicts. When we are angry, the words we use generally confuse the situation instead of telling how we really feel."[4]

As I mentioned before, when a conflict erupts, it is often easier for an observer to understand what went wrong than for those actually involved in the conflict. If two members of your family have frequent misunderstandings, it may be beneficial to pick an objective family member to help the two recognize where they're not hearing each other.

It's the little things piled up on top of each other that build up to big conflicts. If we take care of the small things one by one as they occur, we can ward off the big conflicts — the ones that add up to emotional illness.

Speak the Truth in Love

Though confrontation is important for resolution of differences, *how* we confront another is crucial. We must deal with each other in an attitude of love and not with the aim to hurt. The Bible tells us in Ephesians 4 to speak the truth *in love,* and that is so important. A simple, unimportant disagreement between a husband and wife can be fanned to a major argument by one small remark hurled with the intention to hurt.

When we work at disagreements with an attitude of love, we listen to what the other person needs and try to work things out so we both are satisfied. When we work things out that way, we often find that what we get is better than what we thought we wanted in the first place. Working through a conflict together can actually strengthen the relationship. As James Fairfield says, *"Every* conflict is an opportunity to grow, and we shouldn't hide from it."[5] If we *expect* a better relationship to result from resolving our differences, that will help keep our conflicts from collapsing into shouting matches where everybody loses.

To speak the truth in love calls for the kind of self-giving love that Jesus Christ can bring us. When we open up our lives to Him, we can find this love available to help us — even in times of conflict.

Life is too short...

Chapter 10

*L*ife is too short ...
to live without friends

The web of friendship, woven of varied and colorful threads, binds and frees. "Let there be spaces in your togetherness," said Gibran. Trust frees each to breathe and grow, while weaving a web of common concerns.

WHAT ARE FRIENDS FOR? Sara learned early in life. She had gone to play at her friend's house and was supposed to be home by four-thirty. It was almost five o'clock when she came running home.

Her mother was angry. "Where have you been?" she asked. "You were supposed to be home at four-thirty!"

"But, Mom, I was at Sally's house, you know. I had to stay 'cause she broke her doll."

"That's no excuse for being late. You couldn't fix her doll!"

"No, Mommy, I had to stay and help her cry!"[1]

A friend is to help cry or to help laugh — to talk with and

play with and work with. A friend is to grow with, to give counsel, and to ask advice. A friend is to forgive and be forgiven. A friend is to love and be "at home" with.

I remember friends from very early in my life. At first, a friend was the girl next door, a playmate. We'd meet in the backyard with our toys. By junior high, a friend meant someone to walk to school with and to go to ball games or class picnics with. In high school, friends were to talk with. We talked for hours: about our classes and teachers, and boys, about other girls, about our hopes for the future, and about what made sense in our world.

One of God's good gifts to me has been teachers who are friends. In sixth and seventh grades, one tiny, black-haired teacher turned English and reading classes from "most disliked" subject to "our best" class. She read to us often with her beautiful voice and her dark eyes sparkling. She shared our jokes, clumsy as they were. She cared about the variety of who we were and what we could do. She listened to us and taught us. She was still our friend when her black eyes snapped and her voice became commanding. Friendship made learning more fun, rewarding, and much easier.

Mutual Trust

Charlie Shedd says that "all of us are on a constant hunt for others who will accept our secret selves. We go looking for those who can even stand our ugliness, the rough, unfinished part of us. Of course, we take chances when we expose the inner self. But one who accepts our exposure becomes a candidate for friendship."[2]

Friendship grows as two people feel more and more comfortable together. Another way of saying the same thing is that friends *trust*. We can afford to be honest with our friends because we experience acceptance and trustworthiness.

Someone has said that each of us needs three circles of friends. The first and smallest circle is made up of people with whom we have emotional rapport and in-depth involvement. We see these friends often and share with them our deepest trust. The second circle is a little larger and includes friendships that are enriching. With these friends we share a variety of interests: new books, favorite recipes, crafts, sports, or studies. The more varied the personalities in this circle, the more we are stimulated. The third and largest circle consists of people we want to stay in touch with but people we can't count on for everyday needs.

Perhaps this is a helpful way of analyzing the various needs friends fill. I find it difficult to be that analytical. Somehow friends are people, and they don't fit into categories — even in my mind. But I do agree that friends are essential.

We all want to have friends whom we can trust. We all need friends who will love us through any problem or difficulty, through any new revelation of who we are. Nothing disturbs that trust more than hearing a friend say to us, "I promised her I wouldn't tell anyone, but. . . ." How do we know that what we say to that person won't be repeated, too?

We also want to *be* friends who are worthy of someone else's trust. But how do we say to someone, "You can trust me"? We can only prove it. We can use the difficult times our friends experience to prove to them that we are worthy of their trust.

Since we recently moved into a new community, I've been reminded that close friendships only develop when we are willing to invest time. We can neither learn to know another person nor reveal ourselves without spending time together. With time a friend learns to hear the words that aren't said as well as those that are. And a friend learns to respond to that feeling we can't put into words. Sometimes it is enough to say, "I feel with you." At other times we want insight to get perspective on ourselves or our problem.

A close friend is so comfortable to be with. We blossom,

open up in the warmth of being with close friends. Friends can be quiet together, talk together, play together — without worrying about being misunderstood. As one wrote: "You hear what I'm saying and accept both my tears and my laughter; what I most long for is safely shared with you."

A Friend Is To Help

We can describe friendship in many ways, but probably one of our most common feelings is that a friend is to *help*.

When we want a little advice at income-tax time, we turn to a friend who works with tax returns — if we are lucky enough to have one. When we need help with moving furniture, we turn to a strong-backed friend. When we need a baby-sitter in a crisis, we turn to a friend. A friend is to help.

A friend also helps with cheerfulness, with a steady assurance of faith and hope when we feel uncertain. A friend helps just by staying close through sorrow and loss.

We had neighbors we knew only casually. But one day I learned that they needed help desperately because Edie was scheduled to have a mastectomy, and she had no one to care for her partially crippled husband while she was in the hospital. I offered to help out for two weeks. The week after Edie was home we learned to know each other. She was courageous and spirited, having learned as a child in England that one must face life's changes with determination. One of her gifts was a sense of humor! She could stop and look at herself with a smile — all five feet and one inch of her wrestling with a husband who could not dress himself. And she could tell stories!

Friendship may reach across miles and years. Dorothy McCammon was a missionary in China in the late 1940s. She and a young Chinese woman became friends. As China expelled "foreigners," my missionary friend had to leave. For thirty years she could not communicate with her Chinese friend. One October day in 1978, she received a letter:

Life is too short...

"So many secret memories of our fellowship made my sleepless nights bearable. You have left with me some valuable things to enable me to live through the past twenty-eight years: faith, endurance, and hope. I thank God for friends like you."

A few weeks later another letter reached Dorothy from China. This time her friend told of years of imprisonment. What did Dorothy's friendship mean?

"No, I never once doubted, even in the pitch dark solitary cell, for nineteen months, the love and prayers of my friends. Often you sat very near me, just looking at me with your eyes filled with understanding and love, not making a single sound for fear of the sentinel outside the locked bars. The Lord has such incomprehensible secret ministries and to me, friends like you have sustained me through many crossings over the Red Seas, with courage and strength."

The *power* of friendship — the assurance of continuous caring! How that sustains and heals! How impossible to limit!

Failure and Forgiveness

Friendship is mutual. Sometimes I hear people talk about "being a friend" when what they really mean is "I want to help that person." Of course friends help, but they help each other! One person always giving and the other always taking is not friendship. We may harm the one we wish to help if we encourage an increasing dependence — even in friendship. Friends free each other, encourage each other, help each other to grow.

Of course friends are human. Friends don't always stay with us during the dark times. Friends don't always act unselfishly or know what to do to help. We can't forget that sometimes we all fail.

Jesus made a special point of telling his disciples that He

no longer called them servants but *friends*. But just when Jesus needed His friends most — when He asked them to pray with Him — they fell asleep. When He was taken by the soldiers to trial, His friends ran. But the story doesn't end with betrayal. Jesus forgave his disciples and continued to call them His friends. And they learned to be true friends; the later tests found them strong.

Friendship — loving, trusting friendship — is learned. When Jesus forgave His disciples, He opened the way for their friendship to grow. Our acts of forgiveness will free our friendships to grow and deepen.

Chapter 11

*L*ife is too short ...
to bear grudges or harbor bitterness

Prescription for nursing a grudge: feed daily on the bitter memory, water with repeated tears, harrow the memory with retelling often, shelter from the breeze of hope. So tended, a grudge twists and shapes both conscious and subconscious.

"WHAT IS FORGIVENESS?" Cathy asked her class of handicapped children. One girl answered, "It's when other kids make fun of me because I can't walk ... and instead of being mad, it makes me want to ask God to make them feel good inside, so they don't have to laugh at less fortunate people."

Another child with handicaps said, "Forgiveness? I think it's wanting happiness for someone who once hurt you very badly."

Isn't that a good definition of forgiveness? "Wanting happiness for someone who once hurt you very badly." It sounds simple, but the more I think about it, the more I believe it includes the heart of forgiveness. I can *say*, "I forgive and wish you well." I can even think that I am forgiving the one who hurt me. But to wish that person happiness! How can I do that unless I forgive?

Forgiveness Is Not Easy

Many stories remind me that forgiveness is hard. For twenty-five years Joseph Tucker and his family were missionaries in the country of Zaire. But in the 1960s, revolution swept through Zaire. The village were the Tucker family had lived and worked all these years was captured by the rebel forces; Tucker and other missionaries were seized and imprisoned. Suddenly the fortunes of battle changed, and rescue forces moved back toward the village. Just before the rescuers reached the village, Joseph Tucker was taken out of prison and beaten to death by his captors. It was a painfully torturous execution.

After Mrs. Tucker and her children were rescued and reporters were questioning her, she said, "I understand why these things happen."

The UPI reporter sending this story commented, "In that compassionate sentence you can hear quite clearly the echo of another voice speaking from the cross: 'Father, forgive them; for they know not what they do.'"

Mrs. Tucker forgave her husband's executioners because she understood and loved the people whom she and her husband had served. She knew that long history of injustice, revenge, poverty, and repression that made these rebels fear and hate *all* those who belonged to the oppressor's race.

Few have such a traumatic debt to forgive. And yet, parents are faced with a daughter's rapist/murderer; husbands and wives are asked to forgive a spouse's affair(s); a businessman learns that an employee cheated for years. Whether the debt is large or small, whether this is the first or the third or the tenth time — forgiveness is not easy.

When We Don't Forgive

What if we choose not to forgive? What if we reckon the cost too great?

Let's begin at home. When my husband complains because the milk container is empty (again) or I'm late (again), I can try to get even. After all, he has failings, too. I know the spots where he's vulnerable. We can go on, round after round, each one becoming more vicious. But where will it end? How do two people repair the damage after round ten?

Or I can demand repayment. When my daughter accidentally breaks the treasured antique teapot, I can ask her to pay for a new one. But money will not replace the heirloom. Some losses can be calculated and repaid, but many losses cannot. Even if I say, "I forgive," I can subtly keep reminding her of the debt she "owes" that I expect her to work out by being "extra good." Then her resentment will boil as she feels she has more than paid for her mistake.

Or I can let bitterness and hatred fester, covered with a mask of humility: "I don't count; don't worry about my feelings." But bitterness and hatred take an awful toll on physical and emotional energy. They twist and burn within until I'm not sure whether I hate myself or that other person — until my own self warps to cover and hide the unforgiving cancer.

Forgiveness is costly. But unforgiveness costs even more. To refuse to forgive erodes and finally incapacitates our own ability to accept forgiveness.

How Shall We Be Forgiven?

Two men were talking about forgiveness one day. "But I never forgive when someone wrongs me," one said. "I've a good memory and I never forget or forgive."

The other man looked at him with sympathy: "Then I hope you never do any wrong," he replied.

I have needed — and I do need — forgiveness. I need forgiveness from God, forgiveness from my family, and forgiveness from those I work with. I am dependent on the generous, daily forgiveness of others. Shall I refuse to forgive? *Dare* I refuse to forgive?

Jesus told a parable of forgiveness.

> "Once there was a king who decided to check on his servants' accounts. He had just begun to do so when one of them was brought in who owed him millions of dollars. . . . The servant fell on his knees before the king. 'Be patient with me,' he begged, 'and I will pay you everything!' The king . . . forgave him the debt and let him go.
>
> "Then the man went out and met one of his fellow servants who owed him a few dollars. He grabbed him and started choking him. 'Pay back what you owe me!' he said. His fellow servant fell down and begged him, 'Be patient with me, and I will pay you back!' But he refused; instead, he had him thrown into jail until he should pay the debt. . . .
>
> "The king was very angry. . . ."
>
> Jesus concluded, "That is how my Father in heaven will treat every one of you unless you forgive your brother from your heart." (Matthew 18:23–35 GNB)

Someone has summarized this story with the words: "Forgiven and forgiving are of one piece."

Practicing Forgiveness

· If forgiveness is costly, if it is very *hard* but absolutely necessary, how can I forgive? How can I again wish happiness for one who has hurt me deeply or robbed me of that which was dearest?

As C. S. Lewis says: "Everyone says forgiveness is a lovely idea, until they have something to forgive, as we had during the war. . . . [Now they say] I wonder how you'd feel about forgiving the Gestapo if you were a Pole or a Jew?" And Lewis is honest in his reply. "So do I. I wonder very much. . . . I am not trying to tell you . . . what I could do — I can do precious little — I am telling you what Christianity is. I did not invent it. And there, right in the middle of it, I find 'Forgive us our sins as we forgive those that sin against us.' There is no slightest suggestion that we are offered forgiveness on any other terms. It is made perfectly clear that if we do not forgive we shall not be forgiven. . . . What are we to do?"[1]

How can one learn to forgive? To again wish happiness or pray for blessing on the one who has hurt us?

Along with C. S. Lewis, I think one must begin to *practice* forgiving. Practice on those daily little annoyances: the spilled milk, the fellow employee whose sense of humor makes *you* the butt of his jokes, the parents who forget birthdays and anniversaries. In every family, in every office or shop, along every highway — we find many opportunities to practice forgiving. No home can be happy where forgiveness is not practiced. Children learn to forgive by being forgiven.

Next one can try to *understand*. "Walk a mile (or two) in another's moccasins!" Try to understand the pressures that might make a friend oblivious to other people's feelings. Try to understand the fears that make one strike first. Try to understand past hurts that have twisted a mind until "wrong" may appear "right."

One friend said she asks herself, "Lord, what do *You* think of this person who has hurt me?" Then she can remember again God's love for both.

When we open ourselves to accepting forgiveness, when we *practice* forgiveness, we open the way for God's acts of grace within our lives.

A Test of Forgiveness

In *The Hiding Place* Corrie ten Boom tells of her great test of forgiveness:

It was at a church service in Munich that I saw him, the former S. S. man who had stood guard at the shower room door in the processing center at Ravensbruck [the concentration camp]. He was the first of our actual jailers that I had seen since that time. And suddenly it was all there — the roomful of mocking men, the heaps of clothing, my sister Betsie's pain-blanched face.

He came up to me as the church was emptying, beaming and bowing. "How grateful I am for your message, Fraulein," he said. "To think that, as you say, He has washed my sins away."

His hand was thrust out to shake mine. And I, who had preached so often the need to forgive, kept my hand at my side.

Even as the angry, vengeful thoughts boiled through me . . . I knew Jesus Christ had died for this man. . . . Jesus, I cannot forgive him, I prayed. Give me Your forgiveness. As I took his hand the most incredible thing happened . . . into my heart sprang a love for this stranger that almost overwhelmed me. And so I discovered that it is not on our forgiveness, any more than on our goodness, that the world's healing hinges, but on His.[2]

Why, then, should I forgive? Because forgiving love is like an oil that reduces friction and salves irritation in daily living. Forgive because there is no other way to open the door to healing and reconciliation. Forgive because I know my own frailty. Forgive because God has forgiven me. "Forgive us our sins as we forgive those who sin against us."

Chapter 12

*L*ife is too short ...
to have bedspreads too fancy
to sleep under

"We don't have many guests anymore," the hostess said apologetically. She lovingly caressed the petitpoint on the antique chair and touched the Dresden china tea service. "This is really too valuable to use."

AN ANCIENT MYTH tells of two gods, Jupiter and Mercury, who came to earth disguised as men. They came to test the hospitality of the people who lived on earth. Each person the gods approached was either too busy or unwilling to extend hospitality to the strangers. Only a poor, country couple, Baucis and Philemon, took the two gods in and fed them generously out of the little food they had in the house. Baucis and Philemon were rewarded by the gods who spared their lives but destroyed their stingy neighbors. The couple's cottage was made into a temple, and the two received immortality by being turned into life-giving trees.

Your guests will seldom turn out to be gods or queens or

presidents in disguise, but the point is clear: when we give food, drink, and shelter to one who needs them, we serve God. And Jesus affirmed this in His teachings.

Hospitality Is Fellowship

The Gospel of Luke tells of two sisters, Mary and Martha. When Jesus came to their home for a visit, Martha hurried to the kitchen to prepare the meal. But Mary, just wanting to be with Jesus, stayed with Him instead of going out to help Martha. Finally Martha came to ask Jesus to send Mary to help her. But Jesus reminded Martha that Mary was making a wise choice. Mary needed to sit and talk with Him.

Jesus was not unappreciative of Martha's desire to be hospitable and prepare food for a guest. I think He was saying that sometimes being hospitable means sitting and listening to another's story, being a shoulder for another's tears. Eating together is not the only aspect of hospitality.

Edith Schaeffer writes that "hospitality is not just giving a party. Sometimes it is to be combined with weeping. *Nor* is hospitality just praying with a person and forgetting the physical need of the moment."[1]

Learning to discern the real needs of your guest is one part of hospitality. With practice we gain sensitivity and feel the deeper rewards of hospitality.

Hospitality Is Sharing

Hospitality is sharing what we have. It stems from the heart — an inner desire to lovingly meet the needs of others. True hospitality reaches beyond merely repaying those who have entertained us. It includes sharing with those who need our loving gift of food and home, even though they cannot return the same.

Sometimes spontaneous hospitality is the easiest and most fun. On Easter Sunday several years ago, a widespread ice storm paralyzed our community, leaving us without electricity.

Life is too short...

When we woke to that icy wonderland without electricity, we became creative. One family with a wood stove invited neighbors for an impromptu breakfast of eggs and coffee, cooked on top of their wood stove. Later the three families trooped over to another's home for a Sunday dinner of delicious leftovers from their Saturday-night party. When it was time to pray, the group simply joined hands and gave thanks to God, the Father of all, for keeping everyone warm, safe, fed, and happy!

In a crisis we still respond with genuine, uncomplicated hospitality. During a blizzard, perfect strangers house and feed travelers stranded in the snow. During a storm, one family gave shelter to twenty guests! A few of the guests were returning from grocery shopping, so they shared food all around.

Why does it take an emergency for us to welcome others even when the end tables are dusty?

A number of my friends have visited Third World countries, and each has returned with stories of unbelievably generous hospitality, of being invited to share the very best food a hungry family had to offer. "They were so obviously hungry I could hardly force myself to eat," my friend Pam recalled. "But I knew my refusal would be an insult."

I feel very uncomfortable when I face myself and admit my deepest reasons for withholding hospitality — fear, selfishness, a world centered around me and my needs.

Find Shortcuts

Entertaining guests takes creativity, especially when you work outside the home. I know a few professional women who have all sorts of home-baked cakes, rolls, and casseroles stashed away in the freezer. With the aid of a microwave oven, they are prepared to serve an elegant sit-down dinner for eight — at an hour's notice.

But I don't like to spend my days off in the kitchen! So

to have bedspreads too fancy to sleep under

what do we do when we work full-time and have a wide variety of interests but still like to have friends, family, or strangers over for an occasional meal or gathering?

One suggestion is simply to plan easier meals or parts of meals. Have friends over for just dessert and coffee. Or make a meal of salad or some great soup served with bread and cheese.

If you're expecting company and simply don't have time to make that special cake or salad you want, you may be able to contract the services of an elderly neighbor or relative to bake a special recipe. You could pay the person either with cash, or you could promise a shopping trip or a visit to a mutual friend at a time when you're less busy. This not only provides you with good home-baked things for guests, but it also would give the older person something special to do.

Another way to have friends over "without all the fuss" is simply to ask each person or family to bring one dish to share. This eases the time and financial strain placed on any one couple, but everyone has the same amount of fun.

Another simplifier may be a "come-and-fix-the-food" party. Everyone pitches in to prepare the meal. That one takes planning your space as well as your food! But it can be great fun for an evening.

If you have children, you'll find them eager to help stir up some goody. Of course you may have to deal with cookie batter on the cupboards, but this kind of "on-the-job" training is invaluable for any child. And they will be catching your values — hospitality, caring, and cooperation.

Of course there are still times when you truly want to treat others to a complete meal. You plan ahead, perhaps fixing a dish or two early in the week. Part of your reward in putting out all that energy comes in knowing that they're looking forward to *your* treat, too.

What about cleaning up after you've had guests? It seems to be in vogue to grit your teeth and say, "No, don't worry about the dishes. I'll do them later." And then you face all the cleanup alone; by then it's late, and you're tired. Sometimes I really do prefer to let the dishes go, concentrating my attention and conversation on my guests. But maybe we need to be more willing to accept genuine offers to help out. While washing dishes together, you can talk, laugh, and learn to know each other. Conversation isn't limited by kitchens.

Keep It Simple

If we're trying to practice a simpler lifestyle, we need not put that all aside when company comes. Maybe we're too timid to serve a meatless meal or a simple casserole and salad. I think the best hospitality reflects our everyday patterns. Then we don't become strained or worried about keeping up a "front" that isn't us — or about blowing the monthly food budget in one weekend with expensive foods.

One pastor and his wife often invite to dinner any visitors at church that morning. Before church, she puts a large noodle-meat casserole in the oven. If guests come home for dinner, the children set the large table, open an extra pack of vegetables, make a fresh lettuce or cabbage salad, and serve ordinary sliced bread. These meals are simple and quick but go a long way in welcoming new families to the church. But why should this kind of spontaneous hospitality be practiced only by the pastor and his wife?

Everyday hospitality takes many forms. It can mean a fresh batch of cookies and cold milk for the neighborhood youngsters — even the kid who sometimes bullies your Tommy. It can mean a casserole for a family while a family member is hospitalized. Or it can mean a kettle of homemade soup for the teenagers after a skating party.

Sometimes we may think showing hospitality is just a nice "extra" we do for others — that it's optional and not absolutely necessary. One of the guidelines the Bible gives to Christians is to "practice hospitality" (1 Peter 4:9 REV). Surely that guideline is given as much for my benefit as for the benefit of those to whom I show hospitality. Sharing our food and home, liberally, makes our personalities and lives so much richer!

Entertaining Visitors From Abroad

Each year thousands of visitors come to the United States and Canada. These visitors come from every nation of the world. They may or may not be in agreement with our social, political, and religious philosophies. Most of them have learned some English as a foreign language. They have heard and read about our powerful and wealthy land. They have seen movies of life in America and they come with preconceived ideas of what America is like!

This is our opportunity. We can invite these international guests to visit us in our homes, share a meal, an evening, or even a weekend. Take them along in some daily routine, include them in Sunday's church service, visit a local park. We can help them to understand our daily life. We can share our goodwill and love. In turn, our understanding of the cultures and peoples of the world will broaden.

Ray and Mary have many friends all around the world. I have only met a few of them, but they include a young couple from Lebanon and students from Africa. Their home is alive with momentoes of guests from Japan, Israel, African countries, and Europe. Their guest book includes names and addresses from thirty countries!

Ray is a carpenter and Mary a homemaker. They cannot speak any language other than English. But the language of hospitality is world-wide and understood by all peoples. The warmth of interest and concern for others has universal expressions. As Christians, we consider it a privilege to share God's love with others — to entertain the strangers among us.

Our family enjoyed learning to know international students from India and Japan. We called the university near us, asked for the office for international students, and said we were interested in being a host family. We were invited to a party to meet the two young men assigned to us for that year. From then on we took the initiative and invited them for meals or a weekend visit and especially for holiday celebrations.

They included us too! The Indian New Year's party was great fun. We were introduced to Indian curry and Japanese stir-fried vegetables; we were shown slide shows and given hand-made gifts. We added new words to our vocabularies and made new friends to visit when we travel.

Most colleges and universities have an office to help international guests meet host families. Many other organizations sponsor international guests and look for host families — perhaps for a night, other times for a week or two.

We began by wanting to share with others. We were rewarded by guests who shared with us. A world-wide circle of friends is great wealth!

Reflecting Our Values

Chapter 13

Life is too short ...
to spend much money
on neckties and earrings

Is the choice between earrings or milk for the baby? Between neckties or the utilities bill? What if the baby is my neighbors' or the gas bill is for Uncle Harry? Do neighbors live in Ethiopia or Haiti or Bangladesh?

WHEN SHELLY WAS A LITTLE BOY, he watched his mother carefully scrape the butter wrapper after she had put the stick of butter on the plate. "Why do you do that?" he asked.

"Only rich people throw butter paper away without scraping it," she said. So he knew they were not rich.

The boy grew up; he became a professor and an author, but he always scraped the butter wrappers!

When he was forty, Shelly took a leave from teaching and went to Bangladesh. One afternoon he was trucking bags of powdered milk to a warehouse when he saw a bunch of children following his truck. They were scooping up the small trails of powdered milk that had leaked from the bags. They hungrily licked from their hands those small pinches of milk powder mixed with dust from the city street.

As he traveled into the little villages of Bangladesh, Shelly saw people living on the edge of survival. He wrote a friend:

> These little communities nestled under the palm trees, surrounded by gardens and water ponds, seemed so peaceful and inviting. Yet in their little fields the people eked out a fragile living. They earned less than fifty dollars per person per year, they had no safe supply of drinking water, and not enough food to eat and be full. They had a short life expectancy; little competent medical care. They suffered quietly. They had not butter wrappers to scrape . . . Their desperation crushed my soul!"[1]

For three years Shelly gave himself to the work of increasing food production with fertilizer, new seeds, and some technology.

Now that he's returned to North America from Bangladesh, Shelly knows he isn't rich. "But," he says, "I know I'm not poor!"

I've never had an experience like Shelly's in which I've lived close to people on subsistence levels. However, like Shelly, I've always scraped the butter wrappers. My mother also taught me to preserve garden produce and to use meat sparingly in our diet. So I have some skills to help me cope with the inflation in food costs. I substitute dried beans, peanut butter, cheese for meats. Sometimes I do this grudgingly — it's not fun to be poor. But other times I, too, remember that "poorness" is relative. You don't have to go to Bangladesh or some other far-away country to find those who are poorer. In migrant camps, in cities, in the Appalachian highlands people — including children — are hungry, cold, ill, and without money to buy food or service.

Most of us would find it impossible to eat our usual meals

Life is too short...

while a starving child watched. Can we pretend they have no claims on us because we can't see them? Concern for the poor is at the heart of the Good News — the Christian gospel.

How do we determine how we should spend our money? We need to realize again that we can *choose* how to spend the money we earn. How do we make sure that we spend our funds wisely? How can we use our money in ways that reflect our values? If it is important to us to have money to use for the needs of others, how do we insure that we have the money to give away?

We must reckon with present-day realities. Most families find that food and energy costs take a large percentage of the budget today — even though we try to conserve.

As painful as the process is, we make choices to cut back. And I think it's helpful for families to make those decisions together. What can we do without? How can we "cut corners"? What do we want to save for? How do we want to help others? Perhaps you will have some short-term cuts, some long-range plans, and some creative ways of sharing in your community.

Plan A Budget

Working out a personal or family budget is one way of selecting values and planning ahead. We can't sort out priorities if we spend for "what I want tonight." Quality living means accepting responsibility for choosing realistic goals and working toward them.

If you're like me, I resisted record keeping for years. One time I tried it — tried to account for every penny I spent. And it was a pain! I found it too much trouble and too little reward. But I've learned that I can keep some simple records and set up budgets that really are helpful.

My friend Carol is an example of how anyone can use a budget. Her husband abandoned her just before their little girl was born. Since she had no job skills, she had to go on welfare.

But she knew her only long-range hope lay in getting more education. She applied for help beyond her welfare allotment to go back to school. And then she budgeted. It was really tough living during those years. "But the training was invaluable," she says. "Now I know where to go for second-hand clothes or furniture to help me get along on my minister's salary."

To begin to set up a budget, get check stubs, receipts, and records of income for the past year. First identify the money left *after* income taxes were deducted. That is the amount your family actually could use.

The second step is to find out exactly how you used that money during the past year. Using the check stubs and receipts, sort the expenditures into basic categories to help get a picture.

Sometimes check stubs are only a clue. It takes a lot of recalling to include the check made out to "Sal Freeman" under "housing maintenance." (He was a plumber who fixed the sump pump.)

The whole point of this exercise is to find out how you spent your money during the past year. If you have any other clues, use them. Be sure to include utilities, property taxes, and insurance payments.

Reviewing last year's spending will help you plan. We can be sure that costs and prices will not be less, so you know you'll need just as much — probably a little more — to buy the same commodities and services.

Sometimes this first record of the past year's spending is a surprise. Did we really spend that much money on clothing? Or food? So much was spent in small amounts — a dollar here, two there!

Use Several Checking Accounts

As you look at the record of expenditures, you'll see three categories. Some expenditures are weekly or monthly. Some

Life is too short...

larger ones, such as property taxes, come once a year. The third category is "unexpected."

Just when I find this exercise discouraging, I'm reminded that our skimpiest budgets are more generous than most other people's. A young mother in the Philippines said that her *main* budget items are food and water. The water she buys must be carried in containers for almost a mile.

In *Changing Times* magazine a CPA described his family's financial planning. They maintain two separate checking accounts. In the first account they deposit money to pay for recurring monthly expenses such as groceries, utilities, gasoline, and other household operating costs. In the second account they accumulate funds for expenditures that occur once in a while such as taxes, insurance premiums, and car repairs. They also include in this account money for vacations or household furnishings or other long-range goals.

Of course the key to this plan is to deposit enough money in the first account to meet household expenses and still have enough to put into the second account to be *ready* for the tax bills, the insurance bills, and so on. If you can set it up so that one major bill comes due each month, that helps. Another family adds a third account — money to give. From this account they write checks to their church or to any recognized charitable organization.

Plan Your Budget Together

We've all heard jokes about how women flaunt budgets and spend money recklessly. The truth is, men may also spend money recklessly. And children influence spending. I'm convinced that budget-making should be a family project.

Who keeps financial records and pays the bills? That varies according to interests and skills. Nancy grew up with a father who was a successful businessman. He made the financial decisions and handled family finances. She married an artist who had never concerned himself beyond having enough money to pay for his food, rent, and art supplies.

to spend much money on neckties and earrings   107

The first year was a disaster as Nancy tried to get Don to act like her father. Finally they agreed that she should handle their financial planning. Besides relieving tensions, this arrangement allowed her to budget toward a down payment on a home.

Are music lessons important to you? Plan for your dreams in your budget. If you wish to return to school, if you want to support a needy child, include it in your budget.

Of course budgets are only helpful if they are followed. Ken agreed on a budget, but he couldn't resist mechanical gadgets. Periodically he splurged! Ken and his wife ended up going to a financial counselor who helped them see that each person is responsible if a budget is to work.

A question many parents ask is, "How can I teach my children to use money wisely?" A child learns by *experience* what money will buy, how to save for a larger purchase, and how to relate work to earning. A child may also learn the joy of giving — all as part of family financial planning.

I'm sure that I'm not rich! I'm also sure that I'm not poor! I *am* responsible to use my money in a way that reflects my values. I believe that God is the giver and I'm a "steward" — responsible to carry out His purposes. Money is a servant of life, not a master or a goal.

Life is too short...

Chapter 14

Life is too short ...
to be concerned about whether
towels match bathrooms

The tyranny of "matching things" is like any other thief of one's time and energy. "Therefore do not be anxious, saying, 'What shall we eat?' or . . . 'What shall we wear?' . . . your heavenly Father knows that you need them all. But seek first his kingdom and his righteousness. . . ."   (Matthew 6:31–33 RSV)

BATHROOMS ARE THE CURRENT status symbol in housing, at least in Northern Virginia. "If you want to be the envy of your friends, you'll have a private garden just beyond the glass doors by your marble tub," proclaims one home designer. In the four-color photos, the fixtures as well as the towels, drapes, and rugs all match.

So we move from one image to another in an effort to find happiness and meaning in life. We discard our goal of acquiring a house with a two-car garage and wall-to-wall carpeting for the goal of acquiring a yacht and Persian rugs. But we still miss happiness because we're looking for joy in things rather than in relationships. We put our energy into clothing or housing or cars rather than in caring for people.

A friend of mine wrote a poem that shows how we have gotten so used to discarding and replacing things that we sometimes begin thinking of *people* as disposable.

CONSUMERS' PRAYER

by Joyce M. Shutt

Throwaway bottles
Throwaway cans
Throwaway friendships
Throwaway fans

Disposable diapers
Disposable plates
Disposable people
Disposable wastes

Instant puddings
Instant rice
Instant intimacy
Instant ice

Plastic dishes
Plastic laces
Plastic flowers
Plastic faces

Lord of the living
Transcending our lives
Infuse us with meaning
Recycle our lives.[1]

"Disposable" People

In Washington, D. C., I saw something that disturbed me. Even though I've seen it before and will probably see it again, the sight of a man huddled over a grate on the sidewalk for what warmth he could get from the hot pipes below upset me.

Life is too short...

colic. Intimacy grows between brothers and sisters; they become comrades in a secret alliance against the world. I know we parents sometimes wonder if they'll ever outgrow bickering over who's going to wear whose clothes or who gets the easy chair, but between these normal times of conflict a special kind of sibling loyalty and intimacy develops.

The deepest intimacy takes time — perhaps a lifetime. Friends continually share the experience and communication that reveal oneself to another.

Intimacy doesn't necessarily mean the baring of one's whole soul to a mate or a friend. We can and should reserve private spaces, separate times to restore an inner sense of wholeness and to check our life direction.

When we reject the idea that instinct intimacy is possible, the long, enduring kind becomes even more desirable. True intimacy is worthy of the discipline and energy required. Intimacy feeds the soul and the spirit; it heals hurts and generates new growth.

Plastic Faces

Have you seen artificial flowers that looked so real you wanted to smell them? Even when you touch or smell the flowers, their velvety petals and fragrance imitate reality.

Even though skillfully made, plastic flowers are an imitation. Perhaps it is the vulnerability and the transience of flowers that we treasure as much as their infinite variety of color and fragrance.

Sometimes I even think I'm seeing plastic faces. Walking the streets of any city are people with masks, plastic faces, put on as a barrier. Even on small-town streets and in the country a certain kind of superficial niceness masks the real person.

When I crowd into a packed elevator, with people pressing me on all sides, I think I wear this public mask. A uniformly accepted code of conduct says, "I'm sorry I have to touch you, but *you* know and *I* know it's just because of this crowded elevator, and we can't help it." A plastic bubble surrounds us that lets us touch without being intimate. Each one looks straight ahead and stands woodenly as if there were no one else in the elevator! Many unwritten codes of conduct help us preserve our privacy in the public arena.

But what happens if one forgets to remove that plastic mask? Or worse, what happens if one chooses to keep the barriers always in place? Then all relationships are plastic, too. And the loneliness and alienation that follow become so painful that "plasticizing" internally seems to be the only way of coping.

When you smile, is it a plastic smile, an automatic greeting? Or do you smile meeting the other person's eyes squarely and warmly, with a depth of feeling that's not afraid to show you care?

When I greet my husband after being separated all day, do I show with my face that I'm glad to see him? If I'm upset and angry, can I share what's bothering me rather than hiding it behind a plastic mask? "If you can't tell what's bothering me, than *I'm* not going to tell you!"

Plastic faces, like plastic flowers, are less fragile than the real thing. And so sometimes we use plastic faces to mask our feelings and hide the points at which we can be hurt or healed.

Plastic faces, like plastic flowers are conventions of society: they enable us to parade with something that looks like the real thing but mocks the God-given emotions, expressions, and love we were meant to give and receive.

A plastic face is OK to use in a crowded elevator. But I dare you — dare myself — to take off the mask with the people I live and work with every day.

I want to learn to consciously value the people I meet. I want to challenge ways of thinking, ways of speaking, ways of acting that dehumanize. Students are not numbers to move conveniently from one class to another. The young woman using food stamps in the line ahead of me is not to be categorically dismissed as "one of those." Even those persons who have been sentenced to prison are still persons — not "disposables."

The God who said that even the hairs of our head are numbered loves the *real* person, forgives sins, loves the weak and handicapped, heals scars. He chooses the real over the plastic each time!

Chapter 15

Life is too short ...
to lay waste our earth

I enjoy the early morning — well, not too early. Just a few minutes before the rest of the family wakes up. A glass of juice and a place to sit and watch the early morning sun play on the roofs on the houses as it moves across the valley. The out-of-doors, the earth that is so beautiful, calls us to care for it as well as enjoy it!

"IF WE SELL YOU OUR LAND, WILL YOU LOVE IT?" the Indian chief asked. His tribe had assembled with the white settlers to sign a treaty. The settlers had already taken the land; the signing of the treaty was a formality. But the chief, for whom the city of Seattle was named, used this opportunity to try to tell pioneering whites what the land meant to the native Americans.

> The Great Chief in Washington sends word that he wishes to buy our land. . . . we will consider your offer. For we know that if we do not sell, the white man may come with guns and take our land.

117

How can you buy or sell the sky? The warmth of the land? The idea is strange to us.

If we do not own the freshness of the air and the sparkle of the water, how can you buy them?

Every part of this earth is sacred to my people. Every shining pine needle, every sandy shore, every mist in the dark woods, every clearing and humming insect is holy in the memory and experience of my people. The wind which courses through the trees carries the memories of the red man. . . . Our dead never forget this beautiful earth, for it is the mother of the red man. We are part of the earth and it is part of us. . . . We know that the white man does not understand our ways. One portion of land is the same to him as the next, for he is a stranger who comes in the night and takes from the land whatever he needs. The earth is not his brother, but his enemy, and when he has conquered it, he moves on. He leaves his fathers' graves behind. . . . He kidnaps the earth from his children. . . . He does not care. . . . His fathers' graves and his children's birthright are forgotten.[1]

The chief poured into his speech his people's reverence for all life, their understanding that all life is supported by the beauty and life-giving bounty of the earth. He even reminded them that someday the whites, too, would be overtaken. "Continue to contaminate your bed, and you will one night suffocate in your own waste," he said.

Love the Land

I wonder, what if we had listened to the wisdom of the Indians? What if we had tried to learn from them the rhythms of nature, the respect for the life-sustaining mother earth? What if we had considered their contention that the earth cannot be owned — it can only be used to produce the food that is needed by all, used so carefully that our children and their children will also live joyously? What if we had reverenced God's creation, which challenges us to understand harmonies

Life is too short...

and balance and rhythm? What if we had heard them as they asked, "If we do not own the freshness of the air and the sparkle of the water, how can you *buy* them?"

Would it have inspired us to clean up the exhaust and smoke spewed from factories in the last hundred years? Would we have refused to make lakes and rivers the dumping place for untreated wastes? As we built our cities, would we have kept parks for trees and land for gardens, spaces for people and small animals?

The Indian chief concluded:

> So if we sell you our land, love it as we've loved it. . . . Hold in your mind the memory of the land as it is when you take it. And with all your strength, with all your mind . . . preserve it for your children and love it . . . as God loves us all.[2]

We have loved the land and celebrated its fruitfulness. We love the mountains and the plains, the hills and valleys. But most of all we've loved the money we could make from the land. Greed has stripped the earth in open mines. Greed ravished productive fields. Greed dumped improperly treated wastes. Greed felled the forests and left them barren.

We have chosen to forget that God made the earth to support life. He gave us minds and strength to cultivate and bring it to fruitfulness. God holds us responsible to use it with care, to share with those in need now, and to leave it productive to those who come after.

Choose to Value Our Earth

In recent time new catastrophes have outlined starkly the extent and the results of greed and neglect. Smog blankets cities so that people have trouble breathing. Lead pollutes the air and retards the development of children. Lakes and streams are so clogged and polluted that plants and fish die. Pesticides kill birds. Fuel supplies run short. One after another these crises have come about because we misused our earth (including its air, water, and mineral resources) in the pursuit of wealth.

For example, along the shores of the Great Lakes the largest industrial cities flourished. One big asset was cheap transportation; the raw materials could be shipped across the lakes. Another "asset" was that wastes could be disposed of cheaply. Just dump them into the lake. Some companies spewed millions of gallons of hot water; others dumped chemicals. Cities disposed of all human wastes — sometimes only partially treated — in the lakes.

Finally we noticed what was happening. Fish no longer lived in the lakes. The color of the water changed. The beaches had to be closed. One of the lakes, Lake Erie, was "dying," they said. Environmentalists lobbied until the government ordered the factories to begin cleaning up their own wastes. But the environmentalists took a lot of abuse from commercial interests.

One specific thing I remember involved the detergents I used for laundry. One of the serious water pollutants was phosphate, and phosphate was an ingredient in detergents. In fact it was *the* ingredient we considered necessary to keep our white clothes white!

Our county forbade the use of detergents containing phosphate. At first I thought it a little foolish. What difference would household use make in comparison with industrial use? But within a year, the phosphate pollution in the lake was lowered measurably!

How much of the pollution, the waste of resources, could homemakers really do something about? Our homes have become centers of consumption, and women are the chief buyers.

What are the values most important to us? Do we want the whitest wash or a glassy-surfaced floor or colorful food packaging? Do we want plastics and foils, which do not disintegrate, or will we choose biodegradable materials? Are we willing to pay more for unleaded gas? Can we garden without the pesticides that remain in the earth and air?

We have to learn to make responsible choices to keep the air pure so that *all* can breathe. The wastes poisoning water in one town are carried far downstream to affect the water many drink. Most pollutants will remain as hazards for our grandchildren.

What each person uses for himself or herself affects what is available to others. What each family uses affects what their children and children's children will have. What one country consumes affects what the rest of the world can use.

Caretakers of the Land

How we love, care for, and use our land — our idea of ownership — is not just a personal choice. The Indians recognized that they couldn't *own* the land. The biblical word for this concept is "steward." We are stewards, caretakers of God's creation. "The earth is the *Lord's, and the fulness thereof*" (Psalm 24:1, emphasis added).

God created the earth for sustaining life. He gave men and women the charge of caring for it, cultivating and bringing it to fruitfulness. Each generation is given the same task.

Each of us can take small steps — steps toward living responsibly. We can take steps toward caring for our whole earth, caring for all the peoples of the earth, and caring for those still to come.

There was a slogan popular a few years back: "America — love it or leave it." Perhaps it's time now to change that to "America — love it and *save* it." We are "caretakers" rather than "owners."

Chapter 16

Life is too short ...
to work in a room without windows

The first thing each morning, we look out the window: morning stars, a pink dawn, or gray clouds greet us. Each day has a beauty, and I welcome that moment of freedom, that intimation of possibility.

I HAVE VISITED A JAIL where there are no windows. The women who stay for weeks and months never see the sky or hear the rain or are warmed by the sun. From my dear friend who works with these women all the time I've learned that "no windows" symbolizes their lives in many ways.

At one time or another you've probably heard someone say, "I'd like to be as free as the birds of the air. No one tells them when to come in or what they have to do."

Freedom is an elusive quality. What is it? How do we find or experience it? Can windows bring freedom?

The statement "free as the birds" is an interesting one. Of the little we really understand about the habits of birds, one thing seems clear: they are not carefree. Have you ever watched two birds working at building a nest or caring for their young? Have you watched the birds in formation, winging their way north in the spring or south in the fall? Those who study birds closely observe them taking turns leading the wedge and then dropping back. While one regains strength, another takes a turn at leading. It is also apparent that birds return to the same place, year after year. Yes, they are free to fly — some at great heights — but they must keep the discipline of formation and destination.

Throughout history freedom has been sought and paid for dearly. The promise of freedom is alluring to old and young alike. But few are willing to choose the discipline that brings freedom.

"Freedom" is the plea of the teenager trying to break parental restraints. "Freedom" is the cry of the young person rebelling against academic disciplines. "Freedom" is the aching in the heart of the person tied to the daily round of a spirit-deadening routine.

"If I just could get away from this endless routine of housework — get out of the house and get a job and a regular paycheck — then I'd be free," Ann dreams aloud.

"I can't stand these little children one more minute," Carla says. "I'm an artist, and I just dry up when I have to spend all my time taking care of three preschoolers. I want to be free to create!"

Joyce, the waitress, says: "I hate this job. I have to get up by six every morning to be here to serve breakfast to grumpy men on their way to work. They are as miserable as I am at this lonely hour. If only I could be free. . . ."

Three different women, each dreaming of freedom, each seemingly imprisoned by routine. Is there any promise of freedom?

Life is too short...

Who Controls Our Lives?

As I've already mentioned, freedom is elusive — something we may seek for years and never find or recognize. I believe we choose freedom or servitude as we choose our god, our master.

We may choose a master whose disciplines are so akin to our desires and needs that we find freedom. Jesus said that His yoke fits easily; He knows our individual needs. Sometimes we choose a master whose disciplines are hidden behind false promises. As the years pass life feels more and more binding.

Often the choices of "whom we will serve" are made so gradually and amid such distraction that we do not identify the master. Later we find ourselves in subservience, far from where we had dreamed we would be, and far from being free.

Stacy's mother died while she was a high-school student. Stacy's father was very authoritarian and had never really been her friend; home became a lonely place for her. In her frustration, she turned to her boyfriend for the companionship she was missing. At seventeen she married, looking for freedom and love.

With only a high-school diploma and no job skills, neither Stacy nor her husband were able to get good jobs. Stacy soon became pregnant. Before her nineteenth birthday she was a mother. Her husband already hated his job and was struggling to keep the rent paid, meet hospital bills, and buy food. Their marriage broke up and Stacy once more felt trapped. The freedom she had sought as a teenaged girl at home was now further from her reach.

Discipline — The Road to Freedom

Think of a musician and the discipline of practice that is necessary to play and make music. I've tried to play the piano a little bit. But my fingers are awkward and untrained, and I cannot translate the music I feel into my fingers. But my daughter, who has practiced piano for years, has fingers so disciplined that they are free to play — to make music!

Perhaps the athlete is a more familiar example. Why should the professional athlete spend so much time in practice? He or she already excels in skills. Practice is necessary because only through practice is discipline learned so that during a game the athlete can play creatively — with freedom.

Madeleine L'Engle said that she chose to marry, believing that freedom lay in the commitment of those vows. "I had made a lot of mistakes and failures in love already, and had learned that structure and discipline were essential in my life if I wanted the freedom to write. . . . After all these years I am just beginning to understand the freedom that . . . making a lifelong commitment to one person gives each of us."[1]

I could use a myriad of other illustrations. Only discipline — inner, self-directed discipline to meet individual needs — is the road to freedom.

Some of the *natural* disciplines of the past — the needs for shelter and food — no longer force us into the disciplines to sustain life. We can buy bread from the store if we choose not to bake. We do not need to cut and store wood for the coming winter because heat and light come on with a switch.

Even social guidelines have eased. Divorce seems easier than the discipline of building a marriage. A retirement home for elderly parents requires less discipline than helping them live on their own.

In seeking freedom, we have given up the disciplines of community and relationships. Yes, we may be free — free of responsibility, free to think only of ourselves, free to serve number one. And free to be lonely!

Freedom Balanced by Responsibility

One time when I was a schoolteacher two boys were vehemently discussing their freedom — freedom to occupy the first place in line. They were ready to settle the question with their fists when I stopped them: "Your freedom ends where his nose begins!" This was a way of saying that one's freedom

Life is too short...

must always allow an equal freedom for others. Freedom is balanced with responsibility.

Each of us is responsible to maintain our freedom without usurping the freedom of "others." Balancing these two is difficult, never settled, always shifting. And that is what makes the question of "freedom" difficult.

The freedom of a child to grow and mature normally depends on parents and teachers accepting their responsibility to care for and teach that child.

My freedom to grow personally and to meet the demands of my work depends on my husband's accepting some responsibility in our home. And his freedom to grow and to perform his work depends on my accepting responsibility as well.

But freedom is never static. Two people who choose to live together will find their needs changing, and circumstances change responsibilities.

In looking for escape from responsibility, many want to retreat to a simple society. Elisabeth Elliot lived in the jungle for some time with a primitive Indian tribe "whose style of life looked enviably free," she said:

> They wore no clothes, lived in houses without walls, had no idea whatever of authority, paid no taxes, read no books, took no vacations. But they had a well-defined goal. They wanted to stay alive. It was as simple as that. And in a jungle which can look very hostile indeed to one not accustomed to living there, they had learned to live. . . . They knew what was expected of them and did it as a matter of course.
>
> They asked only "what am I to do this next moment?" If it were to hunt or to make poison for darts, a man did that. If it were to go out and clear a new planting space, a woman did that. Their freedom to live in that jungle depended on a well-defined goal and on their willingness to discipline themselves in order to reach it. No one could "give" them this freedom.[2]

Many saints of times past have sought "freedom" and found they must practice discipline. Some speak of freedom coming when the "inner" and the "outer" person become one.

That is why men and women have been able to write from prison that they are free. Windowless walls do not determine freedom or captivity. The inner spirit, seeking harmony with its Creator and Giver of Life, is not trapped by brick and mortar.

I agree that life is too short to work in a room without windows; it is also too short to miss the freedom of discipline.

Chapter 17

Life is too short ...
to worry about getting ready for Christmas

"A bowl of apples and oranges, another of nuts in the shell, corn to pop and something warm to drink — we plan our Christmas entertaining. Father brings in extra logs for the fireplace" — words from another era, but they remind us again, "Let Christmas come!"

CHRISTMAS CELEBRATIONS are always the most fun (and the most work) when I've helped with the planning.

Our small church celebrates Christmas with a service on Christmas Eve. About two hundred of us crowd onto the benches to sing carols, listen to a chorus, and enjoy the yearly pageant: shepherds in faded bathrobes, angels in tinsel-trimmed gauzy white gowns, Mary in a blue dress and white shawl, Joseph in a nondescript brown robe, and, front and center, a wooden manger holding a baby doll. Each year is similar, yet unique. I love helping the youngsters learn their lines: "Let us go to Bethlehem to see this baby!" The words are the same year after year, but each child accents them differently. Sometimes we add music — recorders playing along with the organ or sweet-voiced children singing "O Holy Night" and "Away in a Manger."

The preparation and practice are fun, and the smiles of the children a great reward, but there is one major problem: getting everything ready takes a lot of time. Often after I'd committed myself to help I would stop to rebuke myself, "Why did you say yes again? You will never be ready for Christmas!"

"Getting ready for Christmas," a measuring stick of success for mothers, has become at least a two-month project for many of us. We begin baking and shopping early — the cookies go in the freezer as we dash out to take advantage of early sales. We decorate both home and office, write letters and cards and send packages by December 1, plan parties, and shop, shop, shop!

Every year frustration drives me to ask, "How can I possibly get ready for Christmas?" I've come to believe that receiving gifts is the secret.

Receiving with Joy

For as long as I can remember, the first rule of Christmas was *giving*. My parents, teachers, and Sunday school teachers all taught that we should give generously, rather than with an eye on what we wanted. (Still, we always had gift *exchanges*.) I should choose gifts that were thoughtful and meaningful to my friends, and I should budget so my money would "reach around." I continue to hear the exhortations to give beautiful gifts, beautifully wrapped.

But a gift demands a receiver as well as a giver. How does one *receive* gifts meaningfully? Is there a way of receiving that multiplies the joy of both giver and receiver? I've come to believe that Christmas comes as we take time to receive our gifts.

When I think of my favorite receivers, I see little children.

Life is too short...

Their eyes sparkle, their feet dance, and their hands reach for the package! No question as to whether or not *they* want a gift!

A child takes a gift with such anticipation and such obvious delight. A child doesn't hesitate, question the value of the gift, or compare it with last year's gift. A child doesn't make mental calculations as to how much you paid for it or what you are expecting in return. A child's thank you is acted out upon receiving the gift.

I knew a woman who was a beautiful receiver of gifts. A child's drawing, balloons and jelly beans, or a valuable book — each was received with delight and thanks. She knew that to accept and value the gift was to accept and value the giver. She never measured her thanks — so much for a little gift and so much for a larger gift. She just let her joy flow!

C. S. Lewis wrote of being "surprised by joy." He said that as a child he experienced an unexpected surge of joy as he looked at a miniature garden. The bittersweet stab of joy returned at moments throughout his youth, but he could never recapture the emotion. He could receive joy as a gift, but he could not earn it; he was surprised by joy, but it eluded his grasp. With C. S. Lewis, we must *receive* joy. It comes at unexpected moments and from innocent givers. To be "too busy getting ready for Christmas" is to run the risk of missing joy. I've found that joy is often dispensed by the child, the lonely neighbor, the woman waiting in the station, or the person with severe handicaps.

Receiving Simplicity and Freedom

An old Shaker song goes:
> 'Tis the gift to be simple,
> 'Tis the gift to be free.

We talk much of freedom. Women and men alike want it. These two lines from the old song affirm that freedom is a gift and remind us that the gift of simplicity — clarity, singleness of purpose — is necessary for true freedom.

Definitions of the word *simple* vary. One meaning is "retarded or half-witted." That is not the simplicity meant in the song. The gift of simplicity that I'm thinking of is the gift of being natural and honest, without mixed motives, like a young child. To be as simple as a child is to be without pretense or artificiality, to be clear and plain.

Most of us can tell a story of how children have embarrassed us by their total honesty — like three-year-old Sherry who turned to her mother during a dinner conversation: "But, Mommy, I don't see Aunt Martha's nose growing longer!"

Our lives grow complicated as we hide our thoughts and motives behind smiling masks. We are more concerned with what others *think* we are than with what we *really* are. "Socialization" includes learning to say what we think others *want* to hear and trying to do what we think will please others.

One day, after ten years of marriage and the birth of two children, Terry found her husband crying — sobbing. When she asked what was wrong, he couldn't tell her at first. They began to recall when they first met and began to date. Joe had dreamed of a marriage and family in which his wife would be a full-time homemaker. She'd love to cook and care for her house. Terry had tried to remake herself to fit Joe's dream, but ten years later, Joe knew the woman he married was not the image in his dream. Terry could not be his model homemaker.

The good part of this story is that both Terry and Joe have matured. They are ready to love the "real" person. They want to take off the masks and put away the expectations of another's dream and be free to receive the gift that the other is.

Simplicity is a gift we cannot receive unless we ask for it, seek it. And here's a switch — no one can give it to us. We must give it to ourselves — be both giver and receiver. Christmas comes to those who seek simplicity.

Receiving Love

Madison Avenue (that anonymous and faceless dictator of beauty and values) defines Christmas as the time to spend money, give costly gifts to those we love. "Show how much you care by choosing the best," which means, of course, the most expensive.

Christmas calls us to *receive* love, receive God's love in the people who touch our lives. Receive love in the gift of a child, in a plea for help, in the touch of a tired hand, in the daily participation of family meals — the breaking of bread.

The story of Christmas, told in the gospel of Luke, is a story of those who *received* love. Mary, a young girl, received love in a promise — the promise of a life created in her and with her, the promise of joy and pain, which are life's fullness. Mary accepted love, became the servant of love. Her song of praise celebrated both gift and giver, and she envisioned a kingdom of love, where the hungry are filled and the humble raised up.

The shepherds in the field heard Good News: your Savior is born today in Bethlehem. In fear (for who knows the cost of such a gift) they hurried to the stable to accept the Christ-child.

Christmas *came* to them, and it comes to us. Madeleine L'Engle says it so beautifully:

> I believe in one way or another we are all meant to receive Him as Mary did. . . . It was a very small gift that God gave us for Christmas two thousand years ago: only a baby: only himself.[1]

One of the saddest contortions of love is giving only to receive — "I'll give you a gift so you will give me one." But unfortunately that is the commercial message that keeps sales figures growing yearly.

Where does the message take root? Little children learn early that smiles and coos bring smiles and hugs in response. However, if they are ever to understand that genuine love is unconditional, they must also learn that tears bring loving care. Too often that balance is lost and children learn instead that love must be earned by being good. As a school teacher I saw too many children afraid to take their report cards home, afraid of rejection. In just a few years they had learned that love must be earned. Yet none of us can deserve love.

To receive God's love is to accept ourselves. If God counts the hairs of our heads, He is certainly aware of the troublesome gray hears of middle age. He loves the teenager whose hair "just won't act right tonight" and the young mother who has no time to fuss with hers. How interesting that God should define His love as concern even for the number of our hairs. How much He cares for us — old and young, thin or heavy, handicapped, lonely, or trying too hard!

Christmas is a time to open ourselves to the gift of love, and Christmas is a gift that comes without the scurry of trying to get ready for it.

Love has its cost. Love teaches us oneness with suffering and pain as well as with joy. Receiving love makes us vulnerable to its loss as well as more open to the gift. The mystery and the marvel of love is its creative power! Let Christmas come.

Notes

Introduction

[1] Lon Sherer, "Bettie; A Friend for All Seasons," Goshen College *Record*, March 3, 1978.

Chapter 1

[1] Author Unknown, "Faith," *Apples of Gold*, Compiled by Jo Petty (Norwalk, Connecticut: The C. R. Gibson Company, 1962), p. 71.

Chapter 2

[1] David Ray, *The Art of Christian Meditation* (Wheaton, Illinois: Tyndale House Publishers, Inc., 1977), p. 26.

[2] *Ibid.*, pp. 41–57.

[3] Dorothy McCammon and Mary Herr, "From Monologue to Dialogue," manuscript, p. 3.

[4] *Ibid.*

[5] Anne Morrow Lindbergh, *Gift From the Sea* (New York: Pantheon Books, 1955), preface.

[6] Harold Rogers, *A Handful of Quietness* (Waco, Texas: Word Books, 1977), p. 12.

Chapter 3

[1] Gay G. Luce and Julius Segal, *Sleep* (New York: Lancer Books, Inc., 1966), pp. 89–92.

[2] *Ibid.*, p. 13.

[3] *Ibid.*, p. 69.

[4]*Ibid.*, p. 53.

Chapter 4

[1]Gail Sheehy, *Passages* (New York: E. P. Dutton and Company Inc., 1974), p. 350.

Chapter 5

[1]Catharine Brandt, *Forgotten People* (Chicago, Illinois: Moody Press, 1978), p. 45.

Chapter 6

[1]David M. Thomas, Ph.D., "Revitalizing Middle-Aged Marriages," *Marriage and Family Living* (April 1983): 18.

[2]"My Point of View: 'The Language That Led to My Divorce,'" *New Woman* (April 1983): 84.

[3]Charlotte Holt Clinebell, *Meet Me in the Middle*, (New York: Harper & Row, Publishers, 1973), p. 126.

Chapter 7

[1]Antoinette Bosco, *A Parent Alone* (West Mystic, Connecticut: Twenty-Third Publications, 1978), p. 6.

[2]*Ibid.*, p. 59.

[3]*Ibid.*, p. 27.

[4]John Drescher, *Seven Things Children Need* (Scottdale, Pennsylvania: Herald Press, 1976), p. 27.

[5]Bosco, *A Parent Alone*, p. 37.

[6]*Ibid.*, p. 78.

Chapter 8

[1]T. Cecil Myers, *Happiness Is Still Home Made* (Waco, Texas: Word Book Publishers, 1969), p. 14.

[2]Vel Shearer, "The Family: A Race to Begin Again," *WMSC Voice* (May 1979): 15.

Chapter 9

[1] James G. T. Fairfield, *When You Don't Agree* (Scottdale, Pennsylvania: Herald Press, 1977), pp. 21–29.

[2] *Ibid.*, p. 24.

[3] Virginia Satir, *Peoplemaking* (Palo Alto, California: Science and Behavior Books, 1972), p. 165.

[4] James Fairfield, interview by Margaret Foth, "Hope for Conflicts," *Your Time Program* #44.

[5] *Ibid.*

Chapter 10

[1] Bobbie Lee Holley, *Person to Person* (Austin, Texas: Sweet Publishing Co., 1969), p. 27.

[2] "Everybody Needs Somebody . . . ," edited by Charlie Shedd, *New Woman*, (February 1979): 54.

Chapter 11

[1] C. S. Lewis, *Mere Christianity* (London and Glasgow: William Collins Sons & Co. Ltd., 1952), p. 101.

[2] Corrie ten Boom with John and Elizabeth Sherrill, *The Hiding Place* (Lincoln, Virginia: Chosen Books Publishing Company, 1971), p. 215.

Chapter 12

[1] Edith Schaeffer, "Hospitality: Optional or Commanded?" *Christianity Today* (December 17, 1975): 28.

Chapter 13

[1] Maynard Shelly, "Ritual of the Wrapper Sets the Style," *Christian Living* (March 1979): 20–22.

Chapter 14

[1] Joyce M. Shutt, "Consumers' Prayer," *The Mennonite* (October 31, 1978): 638.

[2] Richard L. Landrum, "Disposable People and Throwaway Relationships," *The Messenger* (September 1977): 19.

Chapter 15

[1] *Fellowship Magazine,* Fellowship of Reconciliation, November, 1976. Reprinted in *Issues to Discuss,* ed. Levi Miller (Scottdale, Pennsylvania: Mennonite Publishing House, 1979), pp. 76, 79.
[2] *Ibid.*

Chapter 16

[1] Madeleine L'Engle, *The Irrational Season* (New York: Seabury Press, 1977), pp. 42, 46.
[2] Elisabeth Elliot, *Twelve Baskets of Crumbs* (Chappaqua, New York: Christian Herald Press, 1976), pp. 16, 17.

Chapter 17

[1] Madeleine L'Engle, *The Irrational Season* (New York: The Seabury Press, 1977), p. 27.